Walking the Ephesian Road

Seeking the Heart of God in the Ruins of Ancient Ephesus

LANCE THOLLANDER

To Christie

This book is dedicated to Christie Porsch Thollander. Christie, you have been my best friend, my bride, my love, the mother of my children, my co-worker and the best parts of all that it means to have a life partner. We have been through joy and sorrow, grief and wonder, depths and heights and, together, have been constant recipients of the Grace and Goodness of the Lord Jesus. Christie, I am blessed in you as are all who know you.

All my love,

Lance

Chapters

Appendix

Chapter 1

A Sense of History

The sense of history hung heavily in the air. While it surrounded him on every side, Charlie could also sense its call deep inside. He walked down the broad broken marble steps on his way down Curetes Street towards the huge but battered theater. Conflicting emotions swelled within him. This, his first trip to the ancient city of Ephesus in modern day Turkey, was stirring emotions he didn't know he had.

Charlie had become a believer in Christ while at college. The close camaraderie he had experienced living with other Christians during those years remained a cherished part of his Christian identity. In the same way his current bond with the believers he was closest to formed an integral part of his life with God. The freedom and life they found in pursuing Christ together had forged bonds of love that would never die.

In reading the book of Acts and then Paul's letters to the early church gatherings he felt a similar bond with those early Christ followers. Freedom and life leapt off of the divinely inspired pages. The letter to the Ephesians especially stirred his heart, mind and imagination. What had happened in Ephesus that had given rise to such an incredible letter? What was it that Paul taught there that had unleashed such love among the brothers and sisters in Christ?

Charlie knew that the gospel Paul had preached in Ephesus had not only turned the city upside down but had led to churches being planted all over the region and out to distant lands. Now, as he walked through the ruins of the first century city, Charlie wanted the Lord to do it all again. Walking past the ruins of the ancient terraced homes, the temples, the baths and the grand Library of Celsus, a cry rose up in his heart, *"Lord you once were glorified in this city. People gave up their idols in this place to own you as their king. Move again in this ancient land."*

At the bottom of the hill, Charlie reached the large theater in what was once the heart of the city. Over 24,000 people could gather there in Paul's day. Originally built for plays and civic gatherings, it had been modified under various Caesars so that gladiator battles and animal fights could be staged. Was it possible that Paul might even have been referring to such an event when he wrote to the Corinthians, "If I fought with wild beasts at Ephesus, what does it profit me?" No one knows for sure.

As Charlie climbed the huge stairs leading to the stadium's tiered rows, he could almost hear the 2000-year-old echo of a vast Ephesian mob standing in that same arena. *"Great is Artemis of the Ephesians. Great is Artemis of the Ephesians"* they chanted. The huge mob had repeated that for almost two hours when two of Paul's traveling companions, Gaius and Aristarchus, had been dragged into the stadium to stand trial for stirring up the city in the name of Christ. Sitting down on one of the upper row benches, Charlie tried to imagine the scene.

Once again, a sense of wonder rose in him. God had done amazing things in this place. He had used Paul to bring the life changing news of the kingdom of God to this city known as the "First and Greatest Metropolis of Asia." How had that happened in the home town of the Temple of Artemis, a massive worship center to the goddess Artemis? Indeed, that temple was one of the Seven Wonders of the ancient world. Visitors who saw it said the temple was the most beautiful structure on the face of the earth. What heavenly heights had Paul introduced those early believers to that would so grandly stand the tests of time when earthly kingdoms would come and go? Ancient Ephesus with all its glory was gone. But the kingdom of God was still growing all over the earth. Charlie sat back, closed his eyes and imagined the story unfolding.

Chapter 2

Rome 50 A.D.

The year was 50 A.D. The Roman world was in tumult. Aquila and Priscilla, devout believers in Jesus Christ, weren't sure what to do. Aquila was Jewish by birth and hailed from the town of Pontus in what is now northern Turkey. Priscilla's heritage is not as clear. Her name implied Roman citizenship but somewhere in her life journey she had accepted Christ as her Lord and married Aquila. The Emperor Claudius had just ordered that all Jews must leave Rome. Was it because the Jewish believers there were causing too much trouble speaking of their faith in Jesus?

These two Jesus followers had to pack up their successful leather works business. They felt drawn to move to Corinth. The 700-mile journey over land and water likely took them several weeks. It's very possible that other Jewish believers joined them in the trek. These fellow travelers could have very easily formed the nucleus of a new fellowship that soon sprang up in Corinth. Priscilla's name meant respected or honored in Latin and indeed her name is listed first when this couple is mentioned in the Bible. Aquila's name meant eagle. He was a man who had traveled far, already moving in his life time from Pontus to Rome and now Corinth. Eventually they would make their way over to Ephesus where they would make a major impact in the early development of the Christian church.

It was no doubt a blessing for the believers in Corinth to benefit from the presence of these worldly wise and venerable followers of Christ.

Their home and the atmosphere of life and love that were found there became the fertile soil from which fellowships were born throughout the known world.

Corinth was a raw booming metropolis. Located on a land mass that joined northern and southern Greece as well as the Adriatic Sea on the west and the Aegean Sea on the east, commerce flourished there in first century times. The Greek city that sat on this site for hundreds of years had been destroyed in 146 B.C. by the conquering Romans. After lying dormant for 100 years, it was rebuilt by Julius Caesar in 44 B.C. virtually on the same footprint as the old city. The new Roman city grew rapidly and by the time of Priscilla and Aquila's arrival, some 100 years later, was the largest and wealthiest city in Greece. The population was numbered in the hundreds of thousands. With its large temples built in honor of pagan gods, it was also one of the most decadent. One of the temples was said to have had as many as one thousand prostitutes in its employ. The sailors, merchants, travelers and adventure seekers who passed through this crossroads of the world contributed to Corinth's wild reputation. The huge crowds that gathered there every two years for the Isthmian Games, the equivalent of our modern-day Olympics, added to the decadent lifestyle. But, despite all that or maybe because of it, the Lord had his own designs in mind for this worldly place. At least half of the population were slaves brought to serve those with means. Doubtless, there were many living lives of desperation, seeking a way out of their misery.

So it may be, that to Priscilla and Aquila, Corinth presented itself as a land of opportunity: spiritually, for the spreading of the good news of their Lord Jesus, and economically due to the constant demand for tents to house the transitory visitors. Both proved to be true. It didn't take long for their lives to begin bearing fruit in their new environment.

As Charlie sat on his stone bench high above the theater floor in Ephesus looking west toward the setting sun, he thought about the California culture he had grown up in. His home town was well known for its hippie history and the well documented "freedoms" that were known there. "Tune in, turn on and drop out," relating to the drug culture of the time was a well-known mantra. The availability of "sex, drugs, and rock and roll" was widely advertised and drew the attention of pleasure seekers from all across the United States. Had things changed that much from then and there to the atmosphere in first century Corinth? Perhaps not.

Charlie thought back to the first century timeline of events: another well-known first century traveler was also making his way across the Roman world. He would soon find himself in Corinth as well, crossing paths with Priscilla and Aquila.

Chapter 3

Making History in Corinth

A man named Paul, another first century servant of Jesus, had been proclaiming the news of a risen Savior across the Roman world. Formerly the most zealous of Jewish religious leaders, he had had a miraculous encounter with Jesus while on the road to Damascus about 16 years previously. He had changed from being the most famous and ruthless persecutor of Christ followers on the planet to its most ardent witness for Christ. The Jews who he used to represent, now hated him as a traitor. The Roman government also stood against him as civil uproar seemed to follow him wherever he went.

His preaching of the gospel had cost him dearly. He had most likely already been stoned in a synagogue in Arabia, threatened with death and driven out of Damascus, whipped on the island of Cyprus, shipwrecked on the Mediterranean Sea, beaten and nearly blinded in Pisidian Antioch, stoned and left for dead in the Turkish city of Lystra and severely beaten in Philippi. In spite of all that, he had planted churches across Asia Minor and northern Greece. While they, too, were under attack, the churches were growing in numbers and, thankfully, standing firm in their faith in Jesus.

The most serious opposition came from those who felt the foundations of their Jewish faith were being undermined. These defenders of the Law had wreaked havoc on the churches of southern Asia, places like Lystra, Derbe, Iconium, and Antioch. Coming from Jerusalem, these men were telling the believers that simply believing in Jesus was not enough, they must follow Jewish customs as well. To combat that, Paul had already written a letter to the churches in that region, calling the believers back to simple faith in Christ. He exhorted them to live their lives led by the Spirit of Jesus and not the Jewish law. That famous letter today is known as the New Testament book of Galatians. While Paul was weary and beaten down after all he had been through, he set his sights on the city of Corinth, and arrived there not long after Priscilla and Aquila had set up shop.

It didn't take long for Paul, Priscilla and Aquila to meet. They clearly shared kindred hearts of love for Jesus and had already given up much for Him. They joined forces both in ministry and in tent making. This was the beginning of a beautiful friendship. Paul provided a depth of revelation and vision that stirred Priscilla and Aquila's hearts to new depths of devotion to Jesus. The couple provided a loving atmosphere in their home where believers could share the life of Christ together and the church of Jesus could find down-to-earth expression. Though the church there always struggled with worldliness due to the atmosphere all around it, Paul found a sincere and earnest base from which he could make the gospel of Jesus known.

The Synagogue Erupts

As was his custom, Paul began by going to the local synagogue. His practice was to go to those who had the closest claim to and the most knowledge of the plan of God for mankind, his Jewish brethren. Paul talked about the person of Jesus in the synagogue each Sabbath and was, at first, well received. He returned weekly to explain how Jesus was the Messiah that the Jewish people had been promised. This went on for several months. During the week, in order to support himself, Paul worked alongside Aquila and Priscilla as a tentmaker. While working they talked at great length about the things Paul was sharing in the synagogue. "Iron was sharpening iron" as these fervent believers in a living Jesus opened their hearts and lives to one another.

One day Silas and Timothy, two men who had previously joined with Paul in his preaching travels, arrived from Philippi. This church in northern Greece planted by Paul a year earlier, came to be known as one of Paul's favorites. They had a special love for Paul as well. Knowing that Paul typically covered his own expenses, as well as those of others around him, they decided to send a special gift with Silas and Timothy. Paul was greatly moved by their love. But there were problems ahead. Seeing a growing number of Jews starting to abandon some of their legalistic Jewish customs, the Jewish authorities began to vehemently oppose Paul and his teachings.

Paul eventually tired of the constant opposition from the synagogue leaders. Seeing that Gentiles were also believing in Christ in growing numbers, he decided to turn his attention to them and he stopped teaching in the synagogue. He didn't go far, though, setting up shop right next door in the home of Justus, a new Gentile convert to Christ. Making things more dramatic, Crispus, the leader of the synagogue, accepted Jesus and also left, taking his family with him. The opposition to Paul's message only increased.

No doubt Paul was saying to himself, "here we go again." Thinking back on the various beatings he had endured in the previous places he had been, he turned his heart to the Lord for guidance. Mercifully, the Lord Jesus appeared to him in a vision. In the midst of all this opposition, the Lord comforted his heart. "Don't be afraid, Paul," he said. "Go on speaking and do not be silent. I am with you and no one will attack you for I have many people in this city." Encouraged by that heavenly word, Paul continued on for the next year and a half, teaching the good news of Jesus. Home fellowships, modeled on what went on in the home of Priscilla and Aquila, grew up all over the city of Corinth. Jesus was lifted up and the kingdom of God grew.

But the city was not to remain calm. Under Sosthenes, the new synagogue leader, the religious leaders decided to bring charges against Paul. The angry Jews had him brought before the local Roman magistrate named Gallio. They doubtless accused him of calling for allegiance to a different King, not Caesar. This was the same tactic used against the Lord Jesus himself. As Charlie thought about it, he could hear the chants, "Paul's a revolutionary! He's subversive to the Roman government! He must be killed!" Only 20 years had passed since the Pharisees of Jesus' day stood before Pontius Pilate and roared the words, "We have no King but Caesar!" seeking to get the death penalty for Jesus. That day they were successful. This day they were not.

Gallio would have none of it. Consider his words, found in Acts 18: 14, "If it were a matter of wrong or of vicious crime, O Jews, it would be reasonable for me to put up with you; but if there are questions of words and names and your own law, look after it yourselves; I am unwilling to be a judge of these matters." He had them driven out of his presence and had Sosthenes take the beating that was intended for Paul. According to the rest of Acts 18, Paul spent "many days longer" there in Corinth before sensing from the Lord that it was time to move on. Ephesus was waiting…

Chapter 4

A War of Words

That night in his hotel room, Charlie thought more about Gallio's words. As he considered the story told in Acts 18, he opened his heart to the Lord and asked for insight. As he prayed, a question formed in his heart. What was the proconsul referring to when he talked about "questions of words and names?" What name would be pitted against the law? From what name would words of life and freedom spring? Charlie decided to ask an older brother who had been a mentor to Charlie what insights he might have on this question. He wrote to him that night laying out his thoughts. It didn't take long for Charlie to hear back. Here is what his friend wrote:

"Dear Charlie, thank you for asking about these important questions. As I see it, there are two themes intertwined here. First is the reference to "words." One phrase you will see over and over in the New Testament is "the word of God." While in our day we have pretty much equated that phrase with the Bible, in Paul's world, it meant so much more. Here is a fuller way of looking at it.

God is a communicator. He likes to share his heart! In fact, he created this universe through his speaking. "Then God said…" is the hallmark of each day's creative handiwork in Genesis 1. But that was only the beginning. There are close to 260 references in the Old Testament to the "Word of the Lord" being given to God's people. For example, the Word of the Lord came to Adam, Abram, Jacob, Moses, and Joshua, just to name a few of the ones we know about. Amazingly enough, one day the Word came to you and me. We can surmise from Gallio's words that Paul brought the "Word of the Lord" to Corinth, as well.

As mentioned above, in most cases today when we hear the expression "the Word of God," we think of the Bible. We may be encouraged to do such things as "spend time in the Word"; "study the Word"; and "memorize the Word." There's nothing wrong with any of those activities. But if you asked a believer in Ephesus what the Word of God was, their answer would not have been the Bible. The answer would have been Jesus Christ. That is clearly evident from the first words of John's Gospel, "In the beginning was the Word, and the Word was toward God and the Word was God."

Why is this distinction important?

A War of Words

In some measure the struggle between God and his enemy is a war of words. In the Garden of Eden, God instructed his man not to eat of the Tree of Knowledge. Satan showed up and twisted God's words. He started out his conversation with Eve by saying, "Has God said...?" In the war of twisted words, man was deceived. Satan won that battle. God's words were negated. Mankind became infected with sin. It took the death of God's own Son to remedy the damage that resulted.

Contrast that to how the living Word Jesus behaved when he encountered this same enemy in Matthew 4:1-4: "Jesus was led up by the Spirit into the wilderness to be tempted by the devil...The tempter came and said to him, 'If you are the Son of God, command that these stones become bread.' But he answered and said, 'It is written, "Man shall not live on bread alone, but on every word that proceeds out of the mouth of God."'" The weapons in this face-off were not swords but words and the subject matter was food. Jesus was hungry and his enemy thought he could tempt Jesus to follow his advice. But Jesus did not succumb. He had a higher food source than mere bread. His food source was the speaking of his Father within him.

We can see the deeper meaning here. Bread alone cannot give us life. In the broader spectrum, earthly things cannot fully satisfy us. We were designed to be nourished by the words of God. We were designed to draw sustenance by hearing from our heavenly Father. Without that heavenly guidance, we cannot fully live. Jesus knows that too. After his death, resurrection and return through the Spirit, he communicated that to his followers, including Paul. Creation began with the Word. Jesus came to Earth as the Word. According to the Apostle Peter, we begin our life with God through being born again through an imperishable seed, the Word of God.

Watch what happened when God sent Paul and Barnabas out to take the good news to the nations. They started off on the island of Cyprus, speaking in the Jewish synagogues. But the Jewish leaders turned against them and spoke out against their message. Here was Paul's response: "It was necessary that the word of God be spoken to you first; since you repudiate it and judge yourselves unworthy of eternal life, behold, we are turning to the Gentiles'...When the Gentiles heard this, they began rejoicing and glorifying the word of the Lord; and as many as had been appointed to eternal life believed. And the word of the Lord was being spread through the whole region" (Acts 13:46-49).

There's much more to say on this subject, but for now, Charlie, let's simply say that wherever Paul traveled, including Corinth and Ephesus, he lifted up Jesus Christ as the Word of God, able to reveal his Father, God, to us. I am attaching a much fuller picture of the Word of the Lord. I hope it makes sense to you.[1]

Let me also address the issue of the Name of the Lord. When you first meet someone, what is the point of introduction? Naturally, it is that person's name. We want people to know our name. This is no different with our creator God, who put a natural desire in our hearts for relationship with him. So, let's meet this mighty One.

In Genesis 1:1 in the original Hebrew language, He is introduced to us as Elohim. The Scriptures say this: "In the beginning Elohim created the heavens and the earth..." The Hebrew word conveys this meaning: "one Spirit in plural." Our Elohim, the creator God, is one Spirit, but

---

[1] To read the fuller document on the Word of God go to page 65

He is plural. He is Father, He is Son, He is Spirit. Yet, He is One. This is a great mystery, wonderful to consider. There are 32 references to Elohim in Genesis 1 alone and 2500 uses throughout the Old Testament. How important it is that we realize that the God we call on today is our mighty creator Elohim, one God: Father, Son and Spirit! So how does this become personal?

Yahweh, the Special Name of God

In the original Old Testament Hebrew, God is most often called Jehovah or more accurately, YHWH, (pronounced Yahweh). For example, this name was the one revealed to Moses in Exodus 6:2 when God said, "I am the LORD."

What is fascinating is that the Scriptures call God by this name over 6800 times in the Old Testament. That is more than double the use of Elohim. What is truly meaningful is that Yahweh is the most personal name used to refer to God. When the Lord introduced himself to Moses in this way, he was showing that he wanted Moses to know him personally, even intimately. The use of this name, which means I AM, shows us how personal and present God wanted to be with his people. He was not the God who would be something great to them someday or who was something great to them in the past. No, he is the God who is, the God of the present, the God who is with us now.

In the German language there is a formal word for the pronoun "you." The word is Sie. This form of the word is used in business, when meeting people for the first time, or in conversation with those you do not know well. But there is also a personal word for the pronoun "you." The word is Du. When you have become friends with someone or are part of the same family, instead of using the word Sie when talking with them, the word Du would be used.

Our family lived in Germany for several years when our oldest children were young. We will always remember the time it took us to move from a formal relationship with those in our large apartment building to one that was more personal. To do that we joined with them in community activities, informal outings and evenings together. Finally, the day arrived when they hosted a special get-together for us. In that gathering they officially let us know that from then on, we would call each other by Du. We felt honored and warmly welcomed.

In the same way, by using the name of Yahweh, our God moved from Sie to Du with us. We are now warmly welcomed in his presence. You see, Charlie, wherever he went, Paul likely started out with the message of the Lord's Name and how we believers can know him by calling on that name. I am also attaching a much fuller explanation of what all that means. I hope you enjoy it."[2]

Charlie turned eagerly to the fuller explanation his friend had provided. Considering the truths presented there brought a gripping memory to Charlie's mind. He was travelling in a car on mountainous roads in northwest India with his wife, going to visit some believers in Jesus there. After several hours of travel, the passengers stopped at a gas station to refuel. Standing by a concrete edged flower plot, his stomach started to churn. He immediately felt very dizzy and started to collapse. But rather than simply falling to the ground, his body went rigid and his head slammed into the concrete edge of the flower plot, cutting open his forehead. It seemed as if he had been thrown down there by an attacking force. His eyes rolled back into his head and he lay there motionless. Those who saw what happened feared the worst.

His wife immediately fell down next to him and started calling on the name of the Lord. "Lord Jesus, Lord Jesus," she repeated over and over. Others came running over. "Don't let him pass out, throw water on his face," were vague echoes that eventually came to his ears. He lay there in complete peace. "No, I'm fine, everything is going to be OK, let me go," he could remember thinking. Within minutes, he opened his eyes to see his wife, in tears, above him. He knew immediately that in time, everything would be fine. And it was. In thinking back on that experience Charlie was struck again with the power exercised in his direction through his wife's calling on the Lord. All present were thankful that Jesus was the Name that had been on her lips.

---

[2] To read the whole document on the Name of the Lord go to page 75

Chapter 5

Heading for Ephesus

Charlie was excited as he thought about his friend's words. They had touched his heart. He was even more thankful to the Lord for gracing us with the wonder of his Name. He thanked God that the Word of the Lord had come to Ephesus. As he read through the additional material his friend had included, he wondered what other foundation stones he might be asking his friend about as he traced Paul's steps to Ephesus and beyond. It didn't take too long for him to find another.

The year was now 52 AD. Paul had been living in Corinth for close to two years. The time there had allowed him to largely heal from much of the physical suffering he had experienced for the Lord's sake. Though he would struggle with eye problems throughout his life, he felt ready to widen the scope of his gospel efforts. This time he decided not to go alone. He loved watching how Priscilla and Aquila gathered folks around them in their home and made the love of Jesus real to them. He had seen the power of these house fellowships add strength and daily context to the lives of those who came to Christ. He didn't know what lay ahead but he wanted that practical outworking of the gospel to be part of whatever was coming.

So it was that these three friends and co-workers left Corinth and headed east. Ultimately, he was headed to Jerusalem. A new day was about to dawn in the spread of the good news of salvation through Christ and the coming of a new kingdom to planet Earth.

Arrival in Ephesus

The travelers boarded a boat and sailed to Ephesus on the coast of Asia Minor. Along with Paul, Priscilla and Aquila, were Paul's friends and co-workers, Silas and Timothy. Ephesus was another thriving metropolis, perhaps only rivaled by Alexandria, Egypt, as a center of commerce at that time. It was dedicated to the goddess Artemis, known in Rome as Diana, the goddess of the hunt, fertility, and child bearing. It housed some of the first century world's great buildings. The Artemis Temple, known as one of the Seven Wonders of the Ancient World, was the centerpiece. At least twice as large as the Parthenon in Athens, its beauty was stunning to behold. Travelers came from all over the known world to see it, hence its importance as a trade and worship center. For over one thousand years, this temple served as a religious pilgrimage site. The city population numbered close to 250,000 and its numbers swelled far beyond that when every two years, like Corinth, Olympic-type athletic contests were staged there.

Priscilla and Aquila immediately began to look for a place to live where they could also set up their business. Based on their experience in Corinth, they no doubt looked for a large home with a room big enough to house a few guests and hold gatherings. In the meantime, though his eyes were still fixed toward Jerusalem, Paul decided to go to the synagogue and engage the Jews who were gathered there.

As in Corinth, that first encounter hearing of the story of Jesus, the Messiah, peaked the Jewish leaders' interest. "Stay on," they said to Paul. "We want to hear more." But Paul was anxious to complete his journey to Jerusalem and to visit some of the churches he had planted, on the way. "No," Paul said, "but I will return to you later, if God wills." Evidently Paul did have the desire to return. And as we will see, that was also the Lord's desire for him. Saying farewell to Priscilla and Aquila, Paul and his companions continued on their way. It would be a little over a year before Paul returned to Ephesus.

Apollos Shows Up in Ephesus

While Paul was traveling, a Jewish believer named Apollos, arrived in Ephesus. He is simply described as "mighty in the Scriptures" so he must have been quite an orator with great knowledge of the Old Testament. Like Paul, Apollos headed directly to the synagogue and started boldly proclaiming the news of a coming Messiah. But there was a problem. Apollos only knew the story up to the coming of the Messiah. He had received the "baptism of John" which was a baptism of repentance, in preparation for the coming of the Savior. While devoutly holding forth on all he knew, he didn't know the whole story of Jesus' death, resurrection, ascension and return through the Holy Spirit. Word about him spread through Ephesus among the believing community, eventually reaching the ears of Priscilla and Aquila.

Immediately, the couple set out to find the young evangelist. Sitting down with him, they shared the glorious truths that they had so often heard and discussed with Paul. They went over the crucifixion, the resurrection, and the glorious ascension of the Lord Jesus. They talked about the wondrous coming of the promised Holy Spirit to live in the hearts of believers. They went through the Old Covenant, explaining how verse after verse and picture after picture found their fulfillment in the Lord Jesus.

Apollos was dumbfounded. He absorbed it all and rejoiced. He began to fully understand the way of the Lord in its totality. As he learned more about the work of Paul and the growth of the churches in Greece, he felt a desire to see that work and contribute to it. Aquila and Priscilla encouraged him to do so, knowing that he would be strengthened and the young churches would benefit from his speaking gift and boldness. Apollos left soon after with a letter of endorsement from Priscilla and Aquila. He sailed for Corinth, where upon arrival, he carried out powerful ministry among the Jews and believers there.

A Tapestry is Taking Shape

Charlie stopped his mental journey for a moment and thought about the wisdom of God. Several pieces were coming together in Ephesus that would build a beautiful tapestry of the Kingdom of God. The ancient city had been built around providing earthly pleasure of every kind. Little did those there know it was about to become the scene of great spiritual triumph.

Having fulfilled his purpose in Jerusalem, Paul turned his face back toward Ephesus. As he traveled through Galatia on his way there, he had as many as six companions with him. They might have included such men as Titus, Timothy, Gaius, Aristarchus, Secundus, and Sopater. Charlie knew the historical record wasn't perfectly clear about that. But certainly, some of them were with Paul. All but Timothy had come to Christ through Paul's preaching and Timothy had been raised on it. They were all committed to Paul and his gospel. They had all had their faith tested. That gave Paul strength. On top of that, his trusted friends Priscilla and Aquila were waiting for him in Ephesus. By now they had established a solid base of operations and were developing a network of friends. At the least, Paul had to be hopeful about what lay ahead.

Finding Some Disciples

The travelers arrived in Ephesus to a warm welcome from their friends. A small company of believers had started to gather in Priscilla and Aquila's home. These believers were eagerly looking forward to meeting the apostle who had suffered so much for the name of Jesus. As Paul talked with his friends, they shared developments with him as well. He was excited to hear all that was going on. Then something happened that was to change the whole dynamic of the Ephesian work.

The Scriptures simply say, "when Paul came to Ephesus, he found some disciples." We don't know exactly how that happened. Who were these disciples? Again, the record isn't perfectly clear, but it makes great sense that these were recent followers of Christ who had heard Apollos speak and were moved by his forceful presentation. How can we know this? Consider Paul's words to them when they first met, "Did you receive the Holy Spirit when you believed?" That question certainly spotlights the importance the Holy Spirit holds in Paul's gospel. With all of the problems Paul had previously encountered in the churches of Galatia relating to the Holy Spirit, he must have wanted to make sure that understanding who the Spirit is was central to their faith.

Their answer revealed the wisdom of Paul's question, "No, we have not even heard that there was a Holy Spirit." Paul probed deeper. "Into what then were you baptized?" To which they replied, "Into John's baptism." But wasn't that exactly how far Apollos' understanding of the gospel extended when he arrived in Ephesus? Yes, it was. These new converts to Christ, twelve of them in all, likely heard Apollos in the synagogue and had given their hearts to the new faith centered on the promised Messiah. Among them were Tychicus and Trophimus, natives of Ephesus and Epaphras, who hailed from nearby Colossae. But these young seekers had not yet heard the full story.

Paul immediately gathered them together, laid hands on them and prayed for the Lord Jesus, through the Holy Spirit to fill them with the divine life of God. He then baptized them into the Name of the Lord Jesus. The first building block had been laid. Then, in an amazing display of God's presence and power, these new believers began speaking in various languages, exalting the person of Jesus Christ. What a scene! Their lives were changed forever.

Consider the importance of what has happened here. Only four times in the Scriptures is there mention of having new believers "fallen on" by the Holy Spirit. This happened on Pentecost to the apostles in Jerusalem, in Samaria when the apostles Peter and John went there to follow up on the work of Philip, in Ceasarea when Peter prayed for the Gentiles there and now here in Ephesus.

What do these four events have in common? These are all new waves of the Kingdom of God being launched! In Jerusalem it was the foundation of the church there. In Samaria it was verification to the Jews that God loved the hated half breed Samaritans as much as he loved them. In Caesarea it was the opening of the door to the Kingdom to Gentiles. And here in Ephesus it would form the foundation for the launch of the church into the rest of the known world. This would be the first time that neither one of the Twelve nor Paul would be the catalyst for the founding of a new church. The work that would grow from Ephesus would be led by the disciples of Paul, newly called to the task.

When their authority was questioned in days and years to come, they could look back to this day and declare, "We received the Spirit exactly the same way the first 12 did!" Their birthright to preach the Kingdom of God was the same as that of Peter, John, James and all the rest. That was powerful.

Chapter 6

Going to Heaven

So began the work in Ephesus; Paul holding forth to all who would listen, surrounded by strong co-workers, young men whom he had gathered from across the Roman Empire and now these 12 "locals." Where would Paul begin? Surely, he would start by introducing them to the Word of the Lord and the wonder and power of the Lord's Name. But what next? Would it be the problem of our sinfulness and the need for forgiveness? That is where we usually start with new believers. Surely that would be dealt with early on.

As Charlie contemplated these things, he opened his Bible to the letter Paul had written to the Ephesians. He had written this letter some eight or nine years after the church had been founded. Thinking that Paul would start with some foundational thoughts, he was struck by Paul's words at the beginning of the letter, "Blessed be the God and Father of our Lord Jesus Christ, who has blessed us with every spiritual blessing in the heavenly places in Christ." Could it be that Paul would have started in Ephesus by orienting the believers there to the spiritual blessings available to them in the heavenlies in Christ? Would he have immediately drawn them to the nearness of another realm from which they could draw their life as opposed to all the distractions and dead ends of their earthly world? Charlie was also struck by the connection of these opening words to the very opening words of the Scriptures themselves, "In the beginning God created the Heavens and the Earth." In this place of new beginnings would Paul have chosen to start where everything started, with an introduction to the Heavens and its relationship to life here on Earth? Of course, Charlie couldn't know for sure. There were many ways Paul could have developed the gospel message in Ephesus. But the subject intrigued him and he decided to pursue this Heavenly theme. Again, Charlie decided to begin by asking his older friend what thoughts he might have on the subject. Again, he didn't have to wait long before a response came back...

"Dear Charlie," his friend wrote. "You ask some great questions. I love the subject of Heaven or as I like to think of them, the heavens. And, yes, I think you have hit on something here. I believe the reality of heavenly realms and our access to them was a key ingredient of the message Paul brought to those in Ephesus. Let me again generally describe how he might have approached this subject with the Ephesian believers. Of course, we weren't there so we can't really know for sure. But it is fun to consider such things. And, as before, I will attach a longer document that gives more detail.

What if you invited someone to go to heaven with you? Their response might be something like, "Wait," I'm not ready to die." That's because many believe Heaven only refers to a place where believers go when this earthly life is over. But there's far more to it than that. There are over 700 references to "heaven" in the Bible. This is a place that is very important to God. In the Scriptures the word "heaven" is generally written in the plural and should be translated the heavens or the heavenlies. For example, "Our Father, who is in heaven" should be translated, "Our Father who is in the heavens." This invisible realm called the heavens is not simply a future destination for us, but it is God's current location, the invisible realm where he is found and where he reigns.

Many different images come to mind when considering the heavenly realm. Some envision it as a place where angels sit around with harps playing soothing music. Others view it as an eternal worship service. Many envision it as a place where large mansions await the faithful who stroll down broad golden streets. Some may even be afraid that an endless life in heaven will be boring.

In reality, the heavens are far more than what these images present. The heavens are the realm of God's presence, power and authority. But the heavens are not just the place where God lives. We, too, have been seated there in the Lord Jesus. That's why Paul wrote to those in Ephesus, "God raised us up with Christ and seated us with him in the heavenly places." That made the heavens available to them and to us!

How far away then, are the heavens? As a young boy I remember hearing prayers started out in deep, religious tones, "Our Father who art in heaven," or "Our heavenly Father." These opening words made it seem as though the heavens were millions of miles from where I was. I knew God was in heaven and I hoped he was listening. But he seemed very far away, somewhere above all the stars and the planets.

Though I would never admit it, I wondered how a God who was so far away could really get to where I was. I wondered how he could even hear what I was saying. The idea that the heavens are way, way out there is mistaken. Nor is God way out there, either. Such thinking puts a far greater distance between God and his creation than actually exists. "Way out there" is not very accessible. But that's not the case, because God went to great lengths to be here, totally accessible to us.

Paul was an expert in the Old Testament Scriptures. I can imagine him using the story of Jacob to illustrate his point to those Ephesians. I can hear him quoting the story in Genesis 28:11-18, "And Jacob... came to a certain place, and spent the night there; he had a dream and behold a ladder was set on the earth with its top reaching to heaven: and the angels of God were ascending and descending on it; And the LORD stood above it, and said, I am the LORD, the God of Abraham your father, and the God of Isaac: the land on which you lie, I will give it to you and to your seed. Your seed shall be like the dust of the earth .... and in your seed shall all the families of the earth be blessed.... Then Jacob awoke from his sleep, and said, surely the LORD is in this place and I didn't know it...how awesome this place is! This is none other than the house of God, and this is the gate of heaven."

Paul would have explained how Jacob called that place of interaction between God and man, the house of God, the very gate of heaven, that God in heaven was interacting with man on earth. God in heaven was making his will known on the earth. The communication originated in God, but the result was practical blessing on the earth. He would have shown them that if the house of God is the gate between the heavenly realm and earth, then that realm must be nearer than we think. He would have told them of John the Baptizer saying, "Repent for the kingdom of the heavens has come near." And that Jesus himself said, repent: for the kingdom of the heavens is at hand."

When Paul got to Ephesus, he would have explained to them that Jesus Christ embodied the kingdom of the heavens. He knew that it was the Lord's desire for those believers to learn to fellowship with him in heavenly places. He knew that was how Jesus lived on this planet. He went into God for sustenance; he came out to interact with the world. He spoke what he heard his Father saying. He did what he knew the Father wanted him to do. He was a frequent and welcome visitor to heaven. He found sustenance and direction for living in this fallen world. Paul knew that following the Lord's death and resurrection, through the Holy Spirit, those in Ephesus could be frequent and welcome visitors to the heavens. Well, that's enough for now. I hope you enjoy the fuller explanation of this wonderful topic on the attached pages. With love,"

Charlie finished reading his friend's response, then took some time to look through the attached pages on The Heavens.[3] They encouraged him to continuing taking small leaps of faith to engage his Lord in his heavenly domain. He knew such encounters had changed his life. He knew he needed something beyond his own strength and fervency to stand up to the clamoring calls of the world around him. He knew that something was Jesus Himself. And Charlie knew where to find him. Wonderfully, God had sent the Spirit of his own Son Jesus into Charlie's heart, from which place Charlie could cry out, "Abba, Father" and enter into the Lord's heavenly presence.

---

[3] To see the fuller reading on the Heavens go to page 89

Chapter 7

The Temple of Artemis

As he continued to think about life in Ephesus in the first century, there was another subject on Charlie's mind that he felt sure Paul would have presented early on there. The city was dominated by the huge temple of Artemis located a short distance away from the city. This female deity was said to protect the city from the demonic and wicked forces that existed in what they called the cosmic abyss. As "Queen of the Cosmos" Artemis was believed to have authority over all these powers. Her power was invoked through special prayers and magic spells carried out by those initiated into the temple rites. These incantations and spells were the stuff of great mystery, known only to those in her inner circle. So it was that a great air of mystery surrounded Artemis worship, a mystery that to this day has not been deciphered. It had been that way in Ephesus in the first century for over 500 years.

Charlie believed that there was indeed a great mystery at the heart of God's created universe. He was pretty sure it was a foundation stone of Paul's gospel as well. Charlie had little doubt that Paul presented the reality of God's mystery in Ephesus early on. That it was a subject dear to Paul's heart Charlie could tell from Paul's early references to the mystery in the letter that he wrote to Corinth while he was in Ephesus. Further, looking again at Paul's letter to the Ephesians, Charlie could see that Paul referred to it on the first page where he wrote, "In all wisdom and insight he (God) made known to us the mystery of his will, according to his delight, which he purposed in Christ…" There would be several more references to the mystery soon to come in the letter. Paul, who had been blown away by the depth and wonder of this mystery, was not about to let that mystery go undiscovered. He would show those Ephesian converts, old and young, slave and free, male and female, the truth that God's mystery was not just for the select few but for all who wanted to know and enjoy him.

Charlie knew that in simple terms the mystery could be summed up in a few words: Christ in you the hope of glory. But he also knew that this mystery was at the heart of the glorious foundation laid in the lives of those early Ephesian believers. Once again Charlie decided to consult with his friend and see what thoughts he might have on the subject of the mystery of God. Here is what he heard back…

"Charlie, you are pushing all of my favorite buttons. Yes, from what I read, a great mystery was at the heart of Paul's gospel. And why is that? Because mystery is deep in the heart of God. You may think this off the subject but did you know that the best-selling novelist of all time is an English lady named Agatha Christie? Only outsold by the Bible and Shakespeare, this novelist, who lived from 1890 to 1976, sold over one billion books with another billion translated into other languages. What has made her works so popular over the last 100 years?

She wrote of mystery. Her detective novels captured the imagination of people all around the world. She tapped into a core desire that we all as humans share: to see the mysterious brought forward and then explained.

But where did this deep desire come from? From where does the sense that there is a great mystery that needs solving spring?

This sense comes from God Himself.

Within each of us He has planted a deep awareness that we were made for something special, that we are unique in all creation, that we are part of a story much larger than ourselves. That is because He has written the story and placed a mystery inside it. But what is that story? And what is the mystery hidden in the creation of this universe that once understood, helps our lives make sense?

Ah, to bring that to light will take more than just a few brief words. So when you have time, give a read to the attached document. I hope it will bring you joy.[4]"

---

[4] To see the fuller document on the Mystery, go to page 103

It didn't take Charlie long to read through the Mystery manuscript. When he was done, he felt a prayer well up in his heart. "Lord," he prayed, "fill your people with a sense of your wonderful plan to be the seed of Life in us. Show us what it means that you, the source of Life, live inside of us and want to produce your image in us. Show us the amazing depth of the mystery and how you have surrounded us throughout your creation with clues as to your purpose. And use us, Lord, like you used the saints of Ephesus and of old, to reveal to our world, the glorious freedom that we as sons and daughters of the living God, have to live in peace, love and joy before you. Amen."

Charlie continued to think about the glorious elements that came together to form the gospel to the Ephesians. He didn't feel that he had yet plumbed all its riches. Of course, he realized that he may never be able to fully do that. For 2000 years Bible students have been poring over the depths of that letter. But as he read the letter over and considered the context of the book of Acts, he felt that there were a few other subjects he wanted to explore. One of them was Paul's insistence from the start of his ministry to publicly and without apology proclaim the coming of the Kingdom of God. This was evident from Luke's description in Acts 19 of Paul's first few months there. Here is what he wrote, "And he (Paul) entered the synagogue and continued speaking out boldly for three months, reasoning and persuading them about the kingdom of God."

Charlie was sure that this was very risky for Paul and by extension to those around him. There was already a kingdom in charge in Ephesus. It was called the Roman Empire. From England to Africa and from Spain to Syria, one in four of all humans on the planet lived and died under the power of Roman law. Rome had supposedly brought peace to those lands under its rule. The official decree was that they had brought "salvation" out of chaos. It could be said that Rome was the world's first and most enduring superpower. Because of its dominance, the rulers of the empire took to presenting themselves as divine.

At the top of the Roman power pyramid stood the Emperor. The Emperor was also known as the Kyrios, a Greek word meaning the Lord of the world. The coming to power of the Emperor was known in Greek as euaggelion, which meant good news. It's easy to see the similarity between this language and what the followers of Jesus declared. But what was happening in the Roman government was far from stable. While Paul was living in Ephesus, the current Emperor, Claudius, was poisoned by his third wife, Agrippina. This treacherous lady just happened to be the mother of Nero by a previous marriage. Agrippina very much wanted to see her bloodline on the throne. She accomplished that through the murder of Claudius and the coming to power of Nero. This cruel ruler, who would over his lifetime do much evil to Jesus followers, came to power in 54 AD, the same time that Paul was ministering in Ephesus.

So for Paul to lay the foundation of the church in Ephesus on the fact that a new Kingdom had arrived, with Jesus as the Lord of all, was risky, to say the least. Rather than saying Caesar is Lord, Paul was teaching the disciples to confess Jesus as Lord, and to submit to his rule. Paul also boldly proclaimed his message as the 'good news' in contrast to anything that related to the Roman leader.

Paul's teaching in the synagogue went on for three months before some of the Jewish leaders had heard enough. Certain leaders among them began to criticize Paul. No doubt some of them accused Paul of stirring up opposition to Rome and its authority over the lives of those who accepted Christ Jesus as their Lord. This was very familiar territory to Paul. He realized that he had collected all the fruit for the Kingdom of God that he was going to from the synagogue attendees.

But Paul was looking ahead. He had already found another place where he could hold forth. The Lord had laid much more on his heart that he wanted to deliver to the young men around him and the growing number of new believers who were coming to Christ in this great city. Without missing a beat, he took the disciples with him and started teaching in the school of Tyrannus. Some think Tyrannus was a Greek scholastic who rented his facility to Paul in the afternoons when most schools closed up due to the heat. Others think that Tyrannus was a Jew who ran a private synagogue that he allowed Paul to use. In any case, whatever happened there was dynamic. Out of that blessed place disciples were raised up over the next two years who ended up fanning out over the whole of what was known as Asia. They brought the good news of the Kingdom of God in experiential reality to that part of the known world. According to Luke, their good news spread so thoroughly that "all who lived in Asia heard the word of the Lord, both Jews and Greeks."

Wow, thought Charlie. What a story! How awesome it must have been to sit under Paul's teaching there. Charlie loved the whole subject of the Kingdom of God. He was amazed by how deeply the coming of the Lord Jesus was rooted in kingdom language. As a child, he had heard the story of the three wise men coming to anoint the baby Jesus in a manger. But as he had grown older, he realized the way he had been taught the story had eliminated almost of the drama and the tremendous work God had done to create that scenario. He had not known until fairly recently that in fact there was a lot of bad blood between the Romans who ruled Palestine and the Parthians from whom the Magi came. It had been a little over one hundred years before Paul reached Ephesus that the Parthians had won a decisive battle over the Romans in a Turkish town named Carrhae just 700 miles from where Charlie was sitting, killing 43,000 of their solders. The Parthians had even taken over Palestine for awhile before the Romans recaptured it.

Certainly, Paul would have known all that history as well. Being a Pharisee, he had to know the greater story of what happened between the Magi and Herod and the history that brought the wise men to Jerusalem. Charlie had another great friend and mentor who loved all things related to the Kingdom of God. He decided to send his friend an email, wanting to make sure that he had the story straight.

"Dear T.," he wrote, "I'm in Ephesus, doing some thinking about the gospel of the kingdom that was preached here by Paul. Would you do me a favor and let me know if I have the story about the wise men correct? And, if you have any notes on the Kingdom of God that you could share with me, would you send those along as well? Thanks much. Here's what I've got on the Wise Men:

Chapter 8

The Real Story of the Magi

Three wise men on camels carrying gold, frankincense and myrrh, journey from a long distance following a star, to find a baby born in a manger. This is pretty much what most of us have learned about the Magi and the birth of Jesus. But is this the whole story? Or is there much, much more?

Why, for example, would the arrival of three men on camels have caused Herod and all the chief priests and scribes, and indeed, all of Jerusalem, a city of perhaps 75,000 people, to be troubled as Matthew 2:3 describes? And who were these wise men or Magi? And how did they know about that star? And how did they know it was connected to one coming who would be King of the Jews?

First off, how many people might have actually been in the entourage from the East? This was likely a 700-mile journey across what was mostly desert. It would have taken well over a month to make the journey. Soldiers would have been necessary to protect the travelers from marauding bandits. Extra camels and support people would have been needed to carry the food, tents, cooking supplies, water, and everything else needed to travel across the desert. This was the journey of a lifetime for these wise men. No doubt many would have signed up to come. We can only speculate as to the total number of travelers, but it was likely to have been a massive band. Only a large number would have struck fear into the hearts of Herod and all those in Jerusalem.

To add to that, consider the land and history of where the wise men came from. It was called Parthia, at the time, and was the chief rival to Rome for supremacy in the known world. In fact, Rome and Parthia fought wars against each other for control of what is now the Middle East. In 53 B.C., the Parthians delivered one of the greatest defeats the Romans ever suffered in a town called Carrhae in what is today southeast Turkey. Over 40,000 Roman soldiers were killed. In 40 B.C. the Parthians actually controlled the regions that included Jerusalem for a short time.

Then Rome drove the Parthians out, in 39 B.C. and Herod was placed in charge of the region. He continued to have skirmishes with the Parthians and was definitely well known to them. One ancient record states that one of Herod's rivals for power, Antigonus, offered the Parthians a large sum of money to kill Herod. So there is history between Herod and the Parthian army. Is this one reason why Herod would have been "troubled" to see a large caravan of travelers accompanied by a cohort of Parthian soldiers approaching Jerusalem in the Spring of 2 or 3 B.C.?

Now let's consider the Magi. Where did they get their information about the Messiah, King of the Jews? The wisdom gathering of the Magi had its roots in events that took place around 600 years before the birth of Jesus. Young men named Daniel, Shadrach, Meshach, and Abednego, among others, were taken captive by the Babylonian King Nebuchadnezzar in Jerusalem and taken to Babylon. There Daniel had many great adventures. We all know the stories of Daniel and the Lion's Den and the story of the fiery furnace. Then there are the stories of the King's dreams and Daniel's interpretations. Because of these events and his special favor from God, Daniel became the chief wise man in the Babylonian court, serving under such kings as Nebuchadnezzar, Belshazzar, Darius, and Cyrus.

Daniel had a strong heart toward his God, the God of the Hebrews. He shared his faith and knowledge of the one true God with Nebuchadnezzar and all those around him. His stature and wisdom became so great that in the book of Daniel, chapter 2, we read that Nebuchadnezzar elevated Daniel to be the governor of all of Babylon and declared him to be Chief over all the Wise Men in the land. (Daniel 2: 46-48). In other words, Daniel became the Chief Magi of all Babylon.

We can be sure that from that lofty post Daniel began the teaching of the Hebrew Scriptures to all who served under him and came after him. They also would have known of the prophecies delivered by Hebrew prophets like Isaiah that referred to a coming King of the Jews and the current revelations Daniel himself was getting from the Lord. This included the revelation of a princely Messiah that would be coming to the Jewish nation and the general time period in which the promised King of the Jews would be born.

Down through the centuries, the wise men of Babylon became a type of royal priesthood. It was they who anointed kings and prophesied about events to come. As they continued to hold to the teachings of Daniel, the day finally arrived when one of the prophecies came to reality. By that time Babylonia had come to be known as Parthia. As they studied the ancient records, the magi knew the time was near for the promised King of the Jews to be born. When they saw a special star in the sky, they knew the time was at hand. So it was that the wise men from the East loaded up their camels and headed west to find the One whose coming had been prophesied hundreds of years earlier. The light from the heavenly star affirmed their route, confirming to these scholars of both history and the natural world, the spectacular events that were taking place. As the news of their coming reached Jerusalem, Herod was in a panic. Was this another Parthian war party? Why were they here? Herod knew of the power and stature of these wise men. They traveled in royal style. They were clearly men of great purpose.

But they had not come in the name of war. They had come in the name of worship. Consider their earth-shattering words, "Where is He who has been born King of the Jews? For we have seen his star in the East and have come to worship Him." They were not there to war against Herod. They were not there to conduct some kind of peace treaty. They were there to worship the One who had been born King of the Jews.

Of course Herod was troubled. Of course the religious leaders of the day were worried. They had not been doing their homework. They had not been studying the ancient writings that should have prepared them for the coming of the Messiah. Far from it. Herod's reaction was sadly predictable. He was intent on holding on to his own power. The same is true of most of those around him. He deceitfully sent the wise men off to learn more of the promised King while plotting how best to eliminate the threat to his own rule.

Joyfully for them, the wise men found the Christ child, the real King of the Jews, in Bethlehem. They laid their gifts at his feet, and rejoiced in his presence. A vision given to their Chief Magi, hundreds of years before, had become reality. The purpose of their lives on earth had been wonderfully realized. They headed home with great joy in their hearts. The role laid out for them by the Eternal God centuries ago had been realized.

A great drama continued as Herod tried to blot out this threat to his throne. A multitude of young boys died when Herod had all the boys under two years of age slaughtered in the Bethlehem region. A great conflict had erupted on earth's shores. A new King had arrived on Earth to claim the hearts of those who would love him. But there would be tremendous opposition, and the Kingdom would not come without cost.

Charlie sent his email off and waited to hear back. He imagined Paul sitting in a room perhaps close by, surrounded by young eager faces as he told the amazing story of the Magi and the part they played in ushering in the Kingdom of God to planet Earth. He wondered what it would have been like to hear the story from this wizened, ex-Pharisee, schooled in history and the Scriptures. The world they lived in was very little different than that of the magi's 600 years earlier. They would have identified perfectly well with the difficulties of such a journey. Living as they did under the authority of the Roman sword, they would have understood the political dangers of the announcement of a new King. It wouldn't be that long before the current Emperor Nero would be dipping believers in hot wax, hanging them on trees in Rome and lighting them up as human torches. This Kingdom business was serious business indeed. Charlie knew he would never look at a manger in a Christmas time display in quite the same way. A whole new appreciation of what God had done to bring those royal priests to Bethlehem would now accompany that scene.

Charlie was happy to hear back from his friend that the story of the magi was accurate. In addition, he received an attached longer file with this message, "Charlie, here is a brief look at the Kingdom, based on Old and New Testament scriptures for you to look at. Certainly it was a central theme of Paul's gospel. I think you will find some things in there that will surprise you that are related to Kingdom living, things like the Lord's Supper, the original meaning of repentance and what the role of an apostle is. I hope you enjoy it, T."

Charlie immediately opened the attached file and began reading. When he was done, he again turned his heart to the Lord. "Lord Jesus," he prayed, "you are my King. Thank you for your love. Thank you for bringing your kingdom to earth. Thank you that you will make it known to all peoples, tribes and tongues. And thank you that this kingdom, the Kingdom of your love will one day fill all of time and eternity." [5]

---

[5] To read the fuller document on The Kingdom go to page 121

Chapter 9

Meanwhile, Back in Ephesus

Charlie only had a short time left to spend among the ruins of Ephesus. He also planned to visit the site of Colossae and the ruins at Laodicea before returning home.

As he walked among the ancient dwellings, baths and market areas, he continued to consider the story of Ephesus and Paul's influence there. There weren't just the daily teaching meetings in Tyrannus' school to keep the Jesus followers busy. There was work that had to be done to earn income. Most of them had jobs that took them out into the community every day. There was shopping to be done at the agora. There were the evening gatherings that were taking place in more and more parts of the city. Then there were the travelers who regularly came through Ephesus, either for trade or sports events or just to see the great city with its magnificent temple.

Not infrequently some of those visitors in town would meet a believer, and find themselves in one of the meetings of The Way. There, touched by the love that was evident between those present and hearing that Jesus was the source of that love, they would accept the Lord Jesus as their Savior and King. When it came time to head home, these new believers may have asked if someone could come to their city, town or village to share more of the Jesus story there. Paul realized full well that there were those among the believers' ranks who were ready to take on the challenge of being sent out. This would represent a new wave of church growth, started by Jesus in Jerusalem, spread by the Twelve, then by Paul and Barnabas and now by a whole new generation of workers.

One of these young men was Epaphras. He was from the town of Colossae located about 120 miles east of Ephesus on a main trade route. In earlier times it had been a major trading and commerce center but had dwindled in size as cities like Laodicea and Hierapolis grew in stature. It's possible that Epaphras himself was one of those travelers to Ephesus several years earlier. On a trip there he might have easily heard the message of Christ, come to faith in him, and become part of the fellowship there. As he grew in Christ, his family and friends back in Colossae were often on his mind. Finally, the day came when, with Paul's support, he headed east to bring the good news to his home town.

Charlie could only imagine that these young workers would build as Paul did when he laid the foundation in Ephesus. As he re-read the opening words in both Paul's letter to the Ephesians and his letter to the Colossians, he was struck by another theme that must have been part of their training. Indeed, as Charlie looked at every letter written by Paul, these words or words very close to them, were among the first penned, "Greetings from God our Father, and the Lord Jesus Christ."

While these words are so familiar to most believers today that we cruise right over them, the meaning behind them is staggeringly significant. It would have been especially so to those first century believers, many of whom were slaves and the children of slaves. They had no future. They had no hope. They had no inheritance. Now they were the children of the living God! God was their Father. And Jesus Christ, who had been killed, was very much alive and ready to be their Lord!

These thoughts led Charlie back into the Scriptures. He considered how best this subject of being part of the family of the creator God, our Elohim, would have been introduced. The subject of Jesus giving his life to those who believed in Him came up over and over. Charlie decided to once again turn to his mentor for help. "What is so important about the Fatherhood of God that Paul would open every letter by referring to it. Do you have any thoughts on that subject?" Here is what his friend wrote back:

"Dear Charlie, your questions take me all the way back to a ride I took with my 16-year-old son, years ago in California. "Dad, what's it all about? Why are we here?" my son suddenly asked as we drove down a Sacramento street. I caught my breath. How do you craft an instant answer to the eternal question of the universe; especially one that will make sense to a teenager?

At the risk of oversimplifying this issue, the answer to those profound questions is tied directly to an uncomplicated yet profound word...Life. We are here for Life.

But what do I mean by that? Most believers in Jesus are very familiar with the John 10:10 passage, "I have come that they might have life." Jesus told his followers that he had come that they might have life and have it in abundance. The apostle John reinforced this same point when he wrote, "These things have been written so that you may believe that Jesus is the Christ, the Son of God; and that believing you may have life in his name" (John 20:30-31).

Yes, God wants to give us life.

If we are not careful, however, we can overlook the tremendous depth of this truth. Or, worse still, its meaning can be unrelated to our earthly experience or relegated to a distant time of future importance. For example, we may think of the life referred to in John 10 as a quality of life. The Christian life may have been presented to us as a happy life, a life where our sins are forgiven, our basic needs are met, God is on our side and we are on our way to live forever in heaven. Or we may think of it as a life that we will experience in the future, in Heaven with Jesus, when everything will be made new. The Gospel of John reveals what God has in mind. There we learn that Jesus Christ was unique in the entire universe because, "In him was life and the life was the light of men" (John 1:4).

So when Jesus said he had come to give us Life, what was he talking about? While we may assume that everyone breathing has life, John was talking about a totally different kind of life. He was referring to divine life, the life of God, himself.

There was and is a type of life in Jesus that was different than the life that was in anybody else. In Jesus was the divine, supernatural, Spirit life of God the Father. In the light that emanated from that life, the darkness of all mankind became evident.

Consider the best-known Bible verse in the world, "For God so loved the world that he gave his only begotten son, that whoever believes in him should not perish but have eternal life" (John 3:16). When it comes to this verse, believers have often been taught to think, "Okay, that means I believe in Jesus, he forgives my sins and when I die, I'm going to go to heaven. When I get there, I'll live forever in a big mansion on a street of gold." While that may be the perspective of many, God was thinking in a different direction.

What the Lord was talking about is the life that is in him, the type of life that he has. Jesus walked on planet Earth exhibiting perfect wisdom, total authority, power and love. How did he do that? This is the secret of Jesus. In him there is a heavenly life. It's divine life. It's the life of his Father, God. This is the life that is offered to us through Jesus Christ. This is an amazing, mind-boggling offer!

Imagine how that message must have sounded to first century people, most of whom were locked in pagan religion, living in poverty and fear and subject to their Roman overlords. For them to receive the Life of God, have the Living God as their Father and the Lord Jesus as their King was astonishly liberating. No wonder that Paul started off every letter by reminding the readers of their lofty position. There is much to say on this subject. I am attaching a more complete explanation for you to read in your leisure. [6] Blessings,"

A Riot Breaks out in Ephesus

Charlie read through the document his friend had sent. What was written there made great sense to Charlie. The power of that new Life had given rise to amazing developments in Ephesus. No wonder supernatural things were happening there. Charlie went back and reread Acts 19 where it said that "God was performing extraordinary miracles through the hands of Paul." Sick people were healed. Demon possessed people were set free. Even items that Paul touched could be taken elsewhere and healing could happen through them. Charlie thought about how amazing that must

---

[6] To read the fuller document on Jesus our Life go to page 143

have been. Such things had been sadly commercialized in his 21st century world to the point that one didn't really know if the stories of them happening were legit or not. However, having been to Asia a number of times and knowing the stories of many overseas leaders, Charlie had had the opportunity to either see or hear about such things still going on today. But as Charlie thought about it, even in first century Ephesus, there were those who wanted to personally benefit from the Lord's work.

The story was broadly circulated that the sons of a Jewish priest named Sceva, tried to duplicate Paul's work. Though they weren't believers in Jesus they had tried to cast out a demon in the name of Jesus as Paul was doing. But the demon in question wasn't impressed. The demon recognized them as powerless and actually attacked them, beating them up and tearing off their clothes. Wow! That must have made a dramatic impression on all who heard about it. Charlie found it interesting that Luke, the writer of the book of Acts, had chosen to include this story in his retelling of the first century believers. It said two things to Charlie; demons are real, and, if you're going to deal with them, you better believe in the power of the Name of Jesus. The Ephesians didn't seem surprised about the realness of the demons. What amazed them was that Paul's Jesus had authority over them. As Luke makes clear, "this became known to all, both Jews and Greeks, who lived in Ephesus; and fear fell upon them all and the name of the Lord Jesus was being magnified."

Charlie's observation was that in our western Christian culture today, those who lead "healing ministries" sometimes come across as Christian rock stars. Sadly, they often tried to use the healing gift they had to embellish their own name recognition and bank account. While Paul was definitely becoming very well known in the regions around Ephesus, he wasn't too worried about seeing his name in lights. He was more concerned that he would end up on "Wanted" posters.

The possibility of that happening again in Ephesus grew more likely as the gospel continued to spread. Due to the magic cult surrounding the Artemis temple there were many magicians who flocked there. When practitioners of these dark arts began to discover that Jesus was more powerful than whatever they had to offer and indeed offered the real way to reach the Divine God, they too, began coming to the Lord in large numbers. Challenged to give up their old ways, they confessed their evil practices and burned their magic books. Whether this happened over a period of time or on one special day set aside for this purpose we do not know. We do know that this was no small deal. In the currency of their day, these books were valued at 50,000 pieces of silver. Charlie did some figuring based on the value of such a coin in today's world and figured it could be in the $6 to 8-million-dollar range. That was an expensive bonfire.

That loss, plus what the local purveyors of religious Artemis statuary were losing in declining sales caused the next crisis. It was around 57 A.D. The Festival of Artemisia was about to take place. This was an annual spring event in Ephesus. It was the prime sales season for the guild of silversmiths in Ephesus. Because of Paul's influence in all of Asia, there was a noted slump in sales of the Artemis idol. Demetrius, a local tradesman, started doing the math. He realized a lot of money was being lost through the falling sales of Artemis statues. Paul had even gone so far as to claim that gods made with human hands were not gods at all. Imagine the furor that set off. This had to be stopped. Business could dry up completely.

Demetrius called a meeting of the local craftsmen and stirred them up against the believers. The meeting grew into a type of huge political/religious riot. Who will reign in Ephesus? Will it be the Christian God, Jesus, or will it be Artemis? One angry listener started chanting, "Great is Artemis of the Ephesians! Great is Artemis of the Ephesians!" The cry was picked up and soon spread through the crowd. Someone else likely yelled out, "Let's go find this infidel Paul and get rid of him."

That's all it took for things to escalate even more. The angry crowd surged out of the meeting place and marched through the town gathering numbers and strength as they went. Many who heard the cry had no idea what was going on but they weren't going to miss out on the action. Those in the lead headed for the school of Tyrannus to look for Paul. Paul was not there, but to their misfortune, Gaius and Aristarchus, two of Paul's more well-known partners in the gospel, were. The leaders of the huge mob grabbed them and they headed off to the Theater, the only place large enough to contain the thousands and thousands who had joined the throng. By now most of them had no idea what was going on.

"Are we here because of the Jews?"

"Are we here because of the disciples of Jesus, those who follow The Way?"

"Has someone attacked our goddess Artemis?"

"Is there a revolt being planned against Rome?"

Such were the questions likely shouted back and forth.

Then the Jews in the crowd tried to take control. They pushed forward a man named Alexander to try and make their case. Knowing the hatred for Paul coming from the synagogue, Alexander was likely hoping to create greater problems for Paul by distancing the Jews from Paul and his gospel. But when those in the crowd realized that Alexander was a Jew, their anger grew even more. The chant broke out again, "Great is Artemis of the Ephesians. Great is Artemis of the Ephesians!"

The emotion of the crowd was such that this went on for two solid hours. Finally, a town official, the man who handled the registrations for the athletic games in Ephesus, stepped to the front. This man, known to all, was able to quiet the crowd. Thankfully his measured words brought order to the commotion. His words were clear. He essentially yelled out to them in his commanding voice, "Nothing against our Roman law has been done here. If someone wants to bring a case against someone for any reason, let it be done using our court system. This will not end well if the Roman authorities find out we cannot control our people. Go home!" Heeding his words, the massive crowd filed slowly out.

Meanwhile Paul, who had been kept against his will in hiding, couldn't wait to hear the whole story from Gaius and Aristarchus. One thing was clear: it was time for Paul to get out of Ephesus. Everyone agreed with that. So, after an amazing three years there, Paul left for Macedonia, the Roman province to the north of Greece.

Chapter 10

Paul Travels On

In reading over the story once again, Charlie was struck by how the believers in Ephesians were referred to. First he read that the synagogue leaders began "speaking evil of the Way." Later on, the whole Ephesian riot was described as "no small disturbance concerning the Way." Evidently the faith of the Ephesian believers was known as 'the Way." What did that mean, Charlie wondered? The way to where? Or the way to who? This was not a name thought up for those believing in Jesus by Paul. It had already been given to the Jesus followers. This was clear from Acts 9 where it said of Paul's (then Saul's) purpose in going to Damascus, "if he found any belonging to the Way, both men and women, he might bring them bound to Jerusalem." Clearly, it was dangerous to be part of the Way.

Of course, the most obvious answer would be found in Jesus, Himself. "I am the Way," he said, "and the Truth and the Life." Charlie had already done some writing on Jesus being the Truth, or the Reality, as Charlie preferred to think of him, and the Life. But what did it mean for Jesus to be the Way? Again, the Way to where? And the Way to Who? Or the Way to What? What foundational truths were to be found here? Charlie was particularly taken with one aspect; the way to Who? One section of the letter that Paul had written to the Ephesians kept coming to his mind that spoke to this question. Here's what Paul wrote to them, "And Jesus came and preached peace to you who were far away and peace to those who were near, for through Him we both have our access in one Spirit to the Father."

This led Charlie to think about what the apostle Peter wrote to believers scattered across the Roman world, "For Christ also died for sins once for all, the just for the unjust, so that He might bring us to God, having been put to death in the flesh, but made alive in the Spirit."

The first century message was clear. Jesus is our Way to the Father. Through the Spirit he brings us to God. There we experience the wonderful life and the deep love for which we were made. Charlie thought back to a book he had read several years earlier. It was called *"Heaven is Real"* and was the story of a young boy who had had a near death experience. There was one particular exchange in the book that especially moved Charlie's heart. When the young boy was asked later on why he thought Jesus had given him this experience, his answer was simple. "He wanted me to meet his Dad." That answer resonated so completely with the Jesus that Charlie was getting to know. He wants us to meet his Dad. But that's not all, Charlie thought. He is the way out of sin. He is the way into the heavens. He is the way for us to live as believers, facing all that life throws at us. In considering all of this, Charlie felt drawn to take a closer look at Jesus, made alive in the Spirit, as Peter wrote. Who is this mighty Spirit and how do we relate to him?

Charlie was aware that there was a great deal of disagreement in the Christian family on the subject of the Spirit. For several years he had already been doing a lot of thinking, praying and researching on the subject. He knew that there was hardly a more disputed area of thought and experience than that having to do with the Spirit. He had good friends who came down on pretty much every side of the issue on how we should relate to the Spirit and the Spirit to us. He pulled up a document on the Spirit that he had been putting together. As he read over what he had written, Charlie was struck again by the amazing mystery the Spirit represented. He was thankful he didn't have to work it all out in his mind. He was thankful that the promised Holy Spirit had come. And he was thankful that through that Spirit, the Father, Son and Holy Spirit were all One and available to him. What a great God he had![7]

Charlie did some more research on the timeline of Paul's life after Paul left Ephesus sometime around May 57 A.D. It would be about a year

---

[7] To see the fuller document on The Spirit go to page 159

before Paul was in the vicinity of Ephesus again. He would spend that year traveling around Greece and Macedonia, primarily visiting church fellowships that the Lord had raised up through him in his earlier travels. As always, many exciting events took place. Maybe the most amazing one happened in Troas. There during a late-night meeting Paul had brought a young man named Eutychus back to life after he had fallen asleep and fell out of a three-story building to his death. Despite all the adventures, after the nearly three years that he had spent there, Paul's friends in Ephesus were never far from his heart and mind. He was anxious to have some direct contact with them.

Despite being warned against going to Jerusalem, Paul decided to travel there for the Pentecost celebration. In Assos, Paul collected nine of his co-workers to travel to Jerusalem with him. From there they purchased passage by ship to Miletus, 30 miles south of Ephesus. Paul realized he was close enough to ask the Ephesian leaders to come see him. He and his companions disembarked in Miletus. Paul quickly drafted a letter for the Ephesian church. He apologized that he could not come to visit them because he wanted to be in Jerusalem in time for the Feast of Pentecost in late May. He asked that the elders come immediately to Miletus for an important meeting.

When they arrived Paul told the elders of his plans to visit Jerusalem, and his expectation that they would never see him again. He warned them of wolves who would bring in false teachings desiring to steal the church away and take them into a legalistic relationship with the Lord. Paul had seen all this happen before. He charged the elders to feed and guard the church. When they heard these words, the elders wept openly. They hugged Paul over and over and saw him off through their tears. Whatever great truths Paul's gospel had instilled in the hearts of these believers, the greatest thing they carried for Paul was love.

Paul's ongoing saga is well known today. In brief, he did travel to Jerusalem where he ended up being arrested by the Jews for breaking Temple rules. That led to a tribunal before the Roman authorities where the Jewish leaders demanded his death. For his protection Paul was taken to Caesarea where he waited for two years to have his case heard. In order to save himself from lashings, Paul ultimately declared his Roman citizenship and appealed to have his case heard before Caesar in Rome. Paul ended up being taken to

Rome, arriving there early in 61 A.D. Because he was a Roman citizen and due to the uniqueness of the charges against him, he was allowed to have a private apartment with a guard posted outside at all times.

From what Charlie could determine, Paul had stayed in touch with his friends in and around Ephesus. Epaphras was in his home town of Colossae building a solid foundation there as had been laid through Paul in Ephesus. Paul wrote to Epaphras and asked him to come to Rome and bring him news of all that was going on in Asia. Epaphras was excited to do that, arriving in Rome in July. From all that he heard from Epaphras, Paul decided to write two letters, one to the believers in Colossae and another to the believers in and around Ephesus. These letters were written sometime in the Fall of 61 A.D. or early in 62. While Paul would have liked to have sent the letters with Epaphras, the young worker had fallen ill in Rome and could not travel. Paul's young friend Tychicus delivered the letters instead. Many historians believe that after his trial in Rome, Paul was released in 64 A.D. and allowed to travel around the Roman Empire for a short while. Some of them think that he did visit Ephesus one more time before being re-arrested there and taken back to Rome in 66 A.D. Early church tradition has it that Paul was beheaded there on June 29, 67 A.D.

Charlie was deeply moved by the whole story. As he re-read Paul's words to the Ephesian elders and then went back again and read Paul's letter to the Ephesians, he felt strongly that the conclusions he had come to regarding Paul's teachings in Ephesus were reasonable. He saw the case for the Word of the Lord, the Name of the Lord, the Heavens, the Mystery, the Kingdom, Life and the Spirit. Of course, there were many other topics that Paul would have covered in the years that he spent there. But these were the ones that had stirred Charlie's heart the most. As he considered Paul's direct words to the Ephesian believers, he realized there were a few other subjects that he felt deserved attention. These he broadly grouped under two headings: God's Building, The Church: The Body and Bride of Christ, and The Cross.

There were many rich references to the body of Christ in Paul's writings. He hardly knew where to begin in trying to grasp Paul's understanding of the place that the church held in God's heart. The word for church in the Scripture was ecclesia, referring to the gathering or assembly of God's people. In today's world Charlie knew that for many people, the word church referred to a building or denominational affiliation. "What church do you go to?" is one of the first questions believers want to know when they meet other believers for the first time. But for hundreds of years that was not the case. Only when the German word kirche which referred to the building where believers met gave rise to the use of the word church did the meaning begin to change. But Charlie was interested in first things so he turned his attention to try and understand Paul's vision of the ecclesia. He noted Paul's words to the Ephesian elders to "shepherd the church of God which He purchased with his own blood." Paul reminded them that for 3 years he had worked to "build them up" often shedding tears while he ministered among them. Truly this was a man who loved the people of God.

When Charlie turned to the letter to the Ephesians, he could see that the ecclesia was front and center in the mind of Paul. In the first chapter Paul prayed that the believers there would have the eyes of their hearts enlightened so they would know the hope of God's calling, the riches of the glory of God's inheritance in his people. He ended the chapter by reminding the Ephesians that following his resurrection, the Lord Jesus was raised far above all and then given as head over all things to the church, which is his body, the fullness of Him who fills all in all. That word, fullness, immediately caught Charlie's eye. Paul had also used this word earlier in the letter where he wrote in verse 10 that there was a fellowship coming, suitable to the fullness of the times, the heading up of all things in Christ, things in the heavens and things on the earth."

As Charlie did some deeper digging, he learned that the word "fullness" came from the Greek word "complement." He understood that the complement of something was that which when joined with that something formed a perfect whole. In other words, the church was to be the complement of Christ. God in his mysterious wisdom had decided that his Son, Jesus, should have a complement, a Bride, if you will, who would be Christ's perfect match. She would be full of Jesus and show him off to all of God's creation. He would love her with the same love that he was loved with by his Father and she would love him in return. He would be her life and she would be his expression on this earth. What a lofty role for the church to be given.

It pretty much blew Charlie's mind when he discovered that complement was the very same word God used when he said in Genesis 2:18 "It is not good for the man to be alone; I will make a complement suitable for him." From the beginning of creation, the Father had his eye on building a bride for his Son, one who would love him and be filled with his goodness and life. After God had paraded all the animals before Adam to be named, verse 20 says no complement was found suitable for him. That is when our mighty creator God, our Elohim, put Adam to sleep, removed a rib and from that rib built Eve, Adam's complement and brought her to him. Of course, the reality of that first bride, Eve, is the church, the ecclesia.

In Paul's prayer for the saints in Ephesians 3 he prayed that Christ would dwell in their hearts, that they would be rooted and grounded in the Lord's love, so that they could be filled up, to become the whole complement of God. That is the future we face as the church, the ecclesia, the fullness of the body of Christ. What a grand purpose the Lord has for us, his church!

Paul referred to this one more time in the Ephesian letter. In chapter 5 he quoted Genesis 2:24 when Adam was joined with his complement, Eve, "For this reason a man shall leave his father and mother and shall be joined to his wife, and the two shall become one flesh. This mystery is great, but I am speaking of Christ and the church." Charlie thought this was God's eternal purpose in a nutshell: to build a beautiful bride for his Son, one who matched him in every way, being loved by him and loving him in return. No wonder, Charlie thought, that the great meal at the end of time and the beginning of eternity was called the "marriage feast of the Lamb," in Revelation 19.

Charlie felt there was more to be uncovered regarding the church. Once again he wrote to his friends for their insights. When he heard back, he went through the material and put it together in a way that made sense to him. He believed that a greater understanding of the church in God's thinking would move believers toward a deeper love for others in the body of Christ and for Jesus himself. It was certainly Paul's desire to see the members of the body of Christ fall more and more in love with one another and the Lord. And, to his credit, that definitely was a hallmark of the early Ephesians life together.[8]

---

[8] To see the fuller document on The Church go to page 183

Chapter 11

The Importance of the Cross

All of this brought Charlie to his final thoughts on what were some of the great themes that Paul delivered to the Ephesians. What had made the wonderful truths of Paul's gospel a possibility? What had first opened the door to life in God through Jesus Christ? Charlie's mind went back to what was likely the most well-known Bible verse of his generation: "For God so loved the world that he gave his only begotten son that whoever believed in Him should not perish, but have the Life that is eternal." Yes, what opened the door to all that followed was the love of the Father expressed through the sending of his Son, Jesus Christ to die on the cross and redeem us. Charlie knew that the importance of the cross could not be overestimated in the story of God's redemptive plan. Jesus' death on the hill called Golgotha, the Place of the Skull, was the pivotal event of human history.

Charlie knew that this had to be on Paul's mind while he was living in Ephesus from what he wrote to the believers in Corinth. "For I delivered to you as of first importance that Christ died for our sins and was buried and was raised again on the third day according to the Scriptures." Charlie wondered for a moment if he should have begun his laying out of the Ephesian themes with this topic rather than ending with it. After all, in his letter to the Ephesians Paul started off by reminding the believers in verse 7 that "we have redemption in his (Christ's) blood, the forgiveness of our trespasses, according to the riches of his grace." Of course, Charlie realized that the story of the cross and what was produced there ran throughout everything Paul did. These themes were not independent silos standing apart from one another. No, they all overlapped and fed into one another.

Charlie knew that the graphic story of the Lord's death and resurrection helped form the foundation for the churches of Galatia. Paul had written these words to them five years before he ever set foot in Ephesus. "You foolish Galatians, who has bewitched you, before whose eyes Jesus Christ was publicly portrayed as crucified? This is the only thing I want to find out from you: did you receive the Spirit by the works of the Law, or by hearing with faith? Are you so foolish? Having begun by the Spirit, are you now being perfected by the flesh?" Clearly Paul's presentation of the events of the cross were connected to his message of Life in the Spirit. Charlie hoped that whoever came across the writings he was putting together would also see the linkage of one theme to another. They were all parts of one glorious whole, the good news of Jesus Christ and the coming of his Kingdom.

At any rate, Charlie was glad he had decided to take a look at this final subject, the Cross of Christ. For the last time he wrote his friends and asked them for their insights. When he heard back, he took the liberty of putting their thoughts together with his own into one document. As he considered the work of Jesus on the cross and how the Lord brought the power of the cross to bear on the lives on his followers, he could only thank the Lord once more for his wonderful purpose. He was reminded again of Paul's stirring words to the Galatian believers, "But may it never be that I would boast, except in the cross of our Lord Jesus Christ, through which the world has been crucified to me, and I to the world."[9]

If that was to be Paul's final boast, then Charlie felt fine about ending his Ephesian story there as well. He had decided to compile all his thoughts and send them out for friends to read and comment on. If others happened to have a copy fall into their hands, Charlie hoped they would find the material encouraging. He knew this much, the good news preached in Ephesus and throughout the first century world, starting in Jerusalem, reaching into Samaria and then to the utter parts of the

---

[9] To read the fuller document on The Cross go to page 203

earth was glorious and powerful. That good news was still changing lives around the world and would not stop until all "the kingdoms of the world have become the kingdom of our Lord and of His Christ; and He will reign forever and ever" as the apostle John wrote in Revelation 11. "Lord, hasten the day," prayed Charlie, as he laid down his pen for the final time.

Appendix

The Word of God

"In the beginning was the Word…" John 1:1

God is a communicator. He loves to share his heart with those he loves. He began his work with the physical universe by speaking his creation into existence. *"Then God said…"* is the hallmark of each day's creative handiwork in Genesis 1. Though his speaking, each day's activity was put into motion. But that was only the beginning. There are close to 260 references in the Old Testament to the "Word of the Lord" being given to the Israelites. Many of them say, "the word of the Lord came to…" The Word of the Lord came to Adam, Abram, Jacob, Moses, Joshua, Samuel, Nathan, Solomon, Jehu, Elijah, Isaiah, David, Shemaiah, Jeremiah, and Zechariah just to name the ones we know about in the Old Testament. And, thank God, one day the Word of God came to you and me.

For the Old Testament Hebrews God's purpose in doing that was to give them light on what was coming next. For us today, his purpose is to give us new life. 1 Peter: 1: 23 says, *"For you have been born again not of seed which is perishable but imperishable, that is, through the living and abiding **word of God**."* If you are a believer, what happened in your new birth was that the Lord God moved over the darkness and chaos that was your life and declared, "Become light!" And you did. Paul put it this way in Ephesians 5:8, *"For you were formerly darkness but now you are light in the Lord."* We can now say to him, "Thank you for speaking life into me. Thank you for bringing light into my life." The fact that we have been given new life by the Word of God makes a relationship with that Word important to us.

A good place to meet the Word of God is in John's Gospel. *"In the beginning was the Word, and the Word was toward God, and God was the word. He was in the beginning toward God. All came into being through the word, and apart from him nothing came into being that has come into being. In the word was life, and the life was the Light of men. And the light is appearing in the darkness and the darkness grasped it not."* (John 1:1-5). The Word was with God in the beginning, involved in the creation of all things. The Word was also toward God. That is his natural orientation.

When mankind lost the way to the Tree of Life, we also lost our opportunity to be naturally oriented toward the heavenly. Because of that, we are oriented toward the physical, the material, the earthly. Still, sensing there is a greater something out there, we use religious or man-made attempts to get to God. But, with the closing of the way to the Tree of Life, the true way to heavenly realms was closed. Now that door has been reopened in Jesus Christ. As the Word of God, he has come to bring us into the presence of God and orient us toward the Divine.

This Word described by John was so full of creative life that the entire visible and invisible universe was made by him. When this Word spoke, light broke out like a million stars, dispelling utter darkness. This Word was there in Genesis 1 when the foundations of the heavens were laid, when the boundaries of the oceans were set, and when plant, animal and human kind were brought forth. Later John writes, *"The word was in the world, and the world came into being through him and the world knew him not."* This word is a person, Jesus Christ. John goes on, *"To his own the Word came, and those who were his own, accepted him not. Yet whoever obtained the Word, to them he gives the right to become children of God, to those believing in his name who were born not of blood, neither of the will of the flesh, neither of the will of man but of God."*

In most cases when we hear the expression "the Word of God," we think of the Bible. We may be encouraged to do such things as "spend time in the Word"; "study the Word"; and "memorize the Word." When the Word of God is used in this way, it usually refers to the Scriptures.

Many people learn a song in Sunday School that goes like this, "The B-I-B-L-E, yes, that's the book for me, I stand alone on the Word of God, the B-I-B-L-E." Surely the Bible provides a great foundation of our faith. It is interesting to note, however, that if you asked a believer in Ephesus what the Word of God was, their answer would not have been the Bible. The answer would have been Jesus Christ. Why is that important? God has many ways of communicating himself to us. But they all involve his Son. As John wrote in John 1:17-18, "For the law was given through Moses; grace and truth came through Jesus Christ. God no one has ever seen. The only begotten God, who is in the bosom of the Father, he reveals him." Revealing God to you and me is what the Word of God, the Lord Jesus, loves to do.

A War of Words

In some measure the struggle between God and his enemy is a war of words. In the Garden of Eden, God instructed his man not to eat of the tree of the knowledge of good and evil. Satan showed up and twisted God's words. He started out his conversation with Eve by saying, *"Has God said...?"* In the war of twisted words, man was deceived. Satan won that battle. God's words were negated. Mankind became infected with sin. It took the death of God's own Son to remedy the damage that resulted.

Here's how the living Word Jesus behaved when he encountered this same enemy in Matthew 4:1-4: *"Jesus was led up by the Spirit into the wilderness to be tempted by the devil. After he had fasted forty days and forty nights, he then became hungry. The tempter came and said to him, 'If you are the Son of God, command that these stones become bread.' But he answered and said, 'It is written, "Man shall not live on bread alone, but on every word that proceeds out of the mouth of God."'"* The weapons in this face-off were not swords but words. Interestingly enough, in this confrontation, as in the Garden of Eden, the subject matter was food. Jesus was hungry and in a weakened state. The enemy probably thought it would be easy to tempt Jesus to follow his conniving words. But Jesus did not succumb. He had a higher food source than mere bread. His food source was the speaking of his Father within him. That speaking word told him to denounce the words of the tempter.

We can see the deeper meaning here. Bread alone cannot give us life. In the broader spectrum, earthly things cannot fully meet our needs. We were designed to be nourished by the words of God. We were designed to draw sustenance by hearing from our heavenly Father. Without that heavenly guidance, we cannot fully live. Notice that Jesus answers the question as a man, rather than as the Son of God. This is important because if he as a man with God living in him can defeat the enemy by the word of God, then you and I as men and women with Christ living in us can defeat the same enemy in the same way. Just as importantly, if Jesus Christ in his manhood could not live on bread alone, neither can I.

Shortly afterward Jesus began his public ministry. Here's how he started: *"From that time Jesus began to preach and say, 'Repent, for the kingdom of heaven is at hand'"* (Matthew 4:17). The Word of God, Jesus Christ, declared that the kingdom of heaven was available to men and women on planet Earth. In the same way, the Word of God makes known to us the resources of the heavens so that we can draw from heavenly realms and defeat God's enemy. Jesus was the living Word, and he knew the power that his words contained. He knew there was a revolutionary life force in them. That's why he said, *"Therefore everyone who hears these words of mine and acts upon them may be compared to a wise man who built his house on the rock."* (Matthew 7:24). When he spoke, people were drawn to him, made aware of their need for God, healed and cleansed. As he said to his followers in John 15:3, *"You are already clean because of the word which I have spoken to you."* We need cleansing from the dirt that the world throws at us. For that we need to hear from the Lord Jesus. He will wash us with his cleansing presence. That's what happens when we encounter the Word of God.

As Jesus put it in John 14:23, *"If anyone loves me, he will keep my word; and my Father will love him, and we will come to him and make our abode with him."* This does not first and foremost refer to the Ten Commandments. He is not saying that if you are good and keep the rules, God will like you. No, this refers to the things that Jesus was saying to his disciples right then. Listen to what he was saying in verses 18-21, *"I will not leave you bereaved, I am coming to you. Still a while and the world is beholding me no longer, yet you are beholding me. Because I live, you also will live. In that day you shall know that I am in My Father and you in me and I in you. He who has my precepts and is keeping them, he it is who is loving me. Now he who is loving me will be loved by my father and I shall be loving him and shall be disclosing myself to him."* Holding tight to the Word of God leads us into the love of God; into intimate fellowship with the Father and the Son. Such encounters with the Word change us profoundly. That's far better than trying to please God by keeping the Ten Commandments.

The Word as Spirit

Those who met Jesus were amazed at the power and authority of his words. Here are some examples:

Luke 2:47: *"And all who heard him were amazed at his understanding and his answers."*

Luke 4:32: *"…and they were amazed at his teaching, for his message was with authority."*

Luke 4:36: *"And amazement came upon them all, and they began talking with one another saying, 'What is this message? For with authority and power he commands the unclean spirits and they come out.'"*

Luke 8:25: *"They were fearful and amazed, saying to one another, 'Who then is this that he commands even the winds and the water, and they obey him?'"*

It is obvious that Jesus spoke as no other. But what would happen to this powerful Word when Jesus was crucified, resurrected and ascended? What would happen when he was no longer physically present to carry out the thoughts and will of his Father? Jesus' plan was not to substitute his presence with talks about the kind of person he was, the rules we are to live by, and the good deeds we should do until we see him again someday in heaven.

Here is what Jesus said to his followers in John 14:16-18: *"I will ask the Father, and he will give you another Helper, that he may be with you forever; that is the Spirit of truth, whom the world cannot receive, because it does not behold him or know him, but you know him because he abides with you and will be in you. I will not leave you as orphans; I will come to you.*" Jesus Christ, the living Word, would return as the Spirit of Truth, indwell his disciples and lead them from within.

Let me repeat what Jesus said about the Spirit. *"When the Helper comes, whom I will send to you from the Father, that is the Spirit of truth who proceeds from the Father, he will bear witness of Me, and you will bear witness also, because you have been with Me from the beginning"* (John 15:26). And a few verses later in chapter 16, beginning at v. 13, *"But when he, the Spirit of truth, comes, he will guide you into all the truth; for he will not speak on his own initiative, but whatever he hears, he will speak; and he will disclose to you what is to come. He will glorify Me, for he will take of mine and will disclose it to you…A little while, and you will no longer see Me; and again a little while, and you will see Me."* Testify; hear; speak; disclose; it sounds like this Spirit of Truth would be doing a lot of communicating.

Jesus, the Word in flesh, became the Word dwelling in us as Spirit. This Word glorifies Christ; he reveals the will of the Father and guides us into a living relationship with the Lord Jesus. This is the Word of God unleashed to do his creative work. Notice that the Spirit will testify of Christ and we will do the same. That's exactly what happened in Jerusalem and later in Ephesus. The Word of God did not stop flowing with the heavenly ascension of Christ. Here's what happened in the book of Acts: *"And when they* [the disciples] *had prayed, the place where they had gathered together was shaken, and they were all filled with the Holy Spirit and began to speak the Word of God with boldness"* (Acts 4:31). That Word of God was God's message concerning his Son, Jesus Christ. As verse 33 says, *"with great power the apostles were giving witness to the resurrection of the Lord Jesus, and abundant grace was upon them all."*

The resurrected Lord, now living in his followers, continued to broadcast the Word of God. As Acts 6:7 records, *"The word of God kept on spreading; and the number of the disciples continued to increase greatly in Jerusalem."* But it wouldn't stop there. As Jesus said to his disciples before he ascended in Acts 1:8, *"but you shall receive power when the Holy Spirit has come upon you; and you shall be my witnesses both in Jerusalem, and in all Judea and Samaria, and even to the remotest part of the earth."* The Word reached

Samaria in Acts 8 when Philip went to preach there. As the Scriptures tell us, *"Therefore, those who had been scattered went about preaching the word. Philip went down to the city of Samaria and began proclaiming Christ to them"* (Acts 8:4-5). Do we see the connection? Preaching the word is proclaiming Christ and his kingdom. Verse 12 tells us that Philip's message was the good news of the kingdom of God and the Name of Jesus. In Acts 8:14 we read, *"Now when the apostles in Jerusalem heard that Samaria had received the word of God, they sent them Peter and John."* Through the ministry of Peter, John and, later on, Paul and others, this living Word would go out to the ends of the known world.

We see this in Acts 13 when God sent Paul and Barnabas out to take the good news to the nations. They started off on the island of Cyprus, where they preached in the Jewish synagogues. But the Jewish leaders turned against them and started speaking out against their message. Here was Paul's response: *"Paul and Barnabas spoke out boldly and said, 'It was necessary that the word of God be spoken to you first; since you repudiate it and judge yourselves unworthy of eternal life, behold, we are turning to the Gentiles'… When the Gentiles heard this, they began rejoicing and glorifying the word of the Lord; and as many as had been appointed to eternal life believed. And the word of the Lord was being spread through the whole region"* (Acts 13:46-49).

The Word in You

The powerful Word of God is spreading, growing, and giving eternal life to those who receive Jesus Christ. That Word went out into all the earth and one day reached you. Peter described this process in his first letter: *"For you have been born again not of seed which is perishable but imperishable, that is, through the living and abiding word of God. for, 'All flesh is like grass, And all its glory like the flower of grass. The grass withers, and the flower falls off, But the word of the Lord endures forever.' And this is the word which was preached to you"* (I Peter 1:23-25).

Peter let us know that this Word was Christ when he wrote, *'like newborn babies, long for the pure milk of the word, so that by it you may grow in respect to salvation, if you have tasted the kindness of the Lord.*

And coming to him as to a living stone which has been rejected by men, but is choice and precious in the sight of God, you also, as living stones, are being built up as a spiritual house for a holy priesthood, to offer up spiritual sacrifices acceptable to God through Jesus Christ"* (I Peter 2: 1-5).

If you are a believer, the Living Word of God lives in you. You can go to him for drink, for food, for fellowship, and to be built together with others into the house of God. No wonder Paul wrote to the believers in Colossae, *"Let the word of Christ richly dwell within you, with all wisdom teaching and admonishing one another with psalms and hymns and spiritual songs, singing with thankfulness in your hearts to God"* (Colossians 3:16).

Paul wrote the same thing to those in Ephesus when he said, *"For this reason I bow my knees before the Father…that he would grant you, according to the riches of his glory, to be strengthened with power through his Spirit in the inner man, so that Christ may dwell in your hearts through faith; and that you, being rooted and grounded in love, may be able to comprehend with all the saints what is the breadth and length and height and depth, and to know the love of Christ which surpasses knowledge, that you may be filled up to all the fullness of God"* (Ephesians 3:14-19). Christ, the living Word of God, surrounds us with the love of God and fills us up with the fullness of God. That's a powerful Word.

The Word Allows Us to Rest

In the New Testament, Christ is presented to us as the Word of God. He is the one who gives us rest. He is the one who satisfies the requirements of the law in us. He is the one who communicates to us the love, mercy and grace of God. He is the one who takes us out of death and into life. Hebrews 4 says this, *"For the word of God is living and active and sharper than any two-edged sword, and piercing as far as the division of soul and spirit, of both joints and marrow, and able to judge the thoughts and intentions of the heart. And there is no creature hidden from his sight, but all things are open and laid bare to the eyes of him with whom we have to do. Since then we have a great high priest who has passed through the heavens, Jesus the Son of God, let us hold fast our confession"* (Hebrews 4:12-14).

While these verses are often used to refer to the Bible, a closer look reveals that they refer to the Lord Jesus. He is the Word of God, living in us as Spirit and actively carrying out the Father's will in us. He is the one who knows better than we do what is in our hearts, and he is the one who is able to guide us into the truth. Note the wording of verse 14: *"there is no creature **hidden from his sight**, but all things are open and laid bare to **the eyes of him** with whom we have to do."* These verses refer back to the Word of God, a person who is actively interested in who we are and what we are doing. That person is the Lord Jesus. He knows who you are. He knows what you need. He knows where you fall short. Go to him and allow him to speak peace, joy, love and life into your life. Often he will use the words of Scripture to communicate those things to you. They are a powerful tool in his hands.

As we learn to rest in Christ and allow him to do his work in us, the creative power of the Word of God is unleashed in our lives. That's why a following verse encourages us to *"draw near with confidence to the throne of grace, so that we may receive mercy and find grace to help in time of need,"* (Verse 16). Thank God, his Word is full of mercy and grace—just what we need to follow a holy and living Lord. Will it be boring? No! That life of resting in Christ kicks off a whole new level of spiritual activity in our walk with him and in fellowship with his body.

The Sword of the Spirit

In Ephesians 6 Paul encouraged the believers to take up the whole armor of God. He reminded them that we do not struggle with flesh and blood but with the powers of darkness in heavenly places. He conceded that there is wrestling involved but declared we will be able to stand firm, that we will be able to resist and *"extinguish all the flaming arrows of the evil one."* This is our heritage in Jesus Christ. He won the victory over Satan and lives to make that victory real for us.

While we learn to rest in Christ, as God's people we are called to do battle with God's enemy. So what will we need when we are to go out and fight that battle? What is it that will drive the enemy to his knees and lead to his ultimate destruction? For that we will need a mighty weapon. That weapon is the Word of God.

Here is what Paul said to his friends in Ephesus, *"And take…the sword of the Spirit, which is the Word of God."* Paul did not say that the Spirit waves a sword. He said the Spirit is a sword. That sword is called the Word of God. The Word of God, the Lord Jesus, active in creation, made visible in flesh, now in Spirit, is our weapon in storming the gates of hell. What better armament could we ask for? Remember the description of the Word of God in Hebrews 4: living, active, sharper than any two-edged sword, able to discern the thoughts and intents of the heart, and keenly aware of what is going on in your life. This is your Jesus, the Word that you are to turn to and rest in as you move forward in the kingdom work that God has called you to. We need his words to fight the battles that we face.

Keep in mind that this is a corporate calling that we are part of. Paul is addressing the community of believers in Ephesus here, not one individual. This battle takes an army. As important as each of us is, no one of us can put on all that God is. We need the strength of one another. We need our brothers and sisters in Christ to stand with us in living out this life. Paul knew that. That's why he ended this section with these words: *"Pray at all times in the Spirit… be on the alert with all perseverance and petition for all the saints, and pray on my behalf… to make known with boldness the mystery of the gospel"* (Ephesians 6:18-19). The Ephesians were encouraged to go to Christ in their spirits and, energized by him, pray for one another and for Paul as he continued to make known the good news of Christ. This is how the word of God spreads and grows.

A Final Look

Let's take one last look at Jesus Christ. Here is how the apostle John described him in Revelation 19:11-13: *"And I saw heaven opened, and behold, a white horse, and he who sat on it is called Faithful and True, and in righteousness he judges and wages war. His eyes are a flame of fire, and on his head are many diadems; and he has a name written on him which no* *one knows except himself. He is clothed with a robe dipped in blood, and **his name is called The Word of God.** "*

The One whose robe is dipped in blood and whose name is The Word of God is riding out to make the kingdom of his Father a visible and eternal reality. He is calling you and me. Will we ride with him? We have been cleansed by his blood. We have been born again by the living Word. Now we can invite the living Word who is Christ to dwell in us richly. He can bring the reality and love of the Father to bear in our lives. He can put us in the company of others who have a heart to know him. As he does that we can say to him with anticipation...

Yes, Lord, we will ride with you.

The Name of the Lord

"Whoever Shall Call on the Name of the Lord Shall be Saved..."

What is the most important thing you have ever been given? Is it your health, your house, an inheritance? What gift have you been given that you treasure more than any other? Could it be a keepsake from a beloved parent, relative or friend?

As I think about what has been given to us as believers in Christ, one of the greatest gifts we have received is the gift of his Name. The enjoyment of that name opens the door of the Heavens to us and offers us daily access to Jesus. How does this work?

I will never forget that life-changing evening when I intentionally called on the Lord Jesus for the first time. After hearing an older believer in Christ share about the power of calling on the Lord's name and the beauty of his attendant presence, I was determined to give it a try. I walked out onto the small balcony off our living room, turned my heart as best I knew how in the Lord's direction, and confessed his name out loud; Jesus, Lord. As I quietly waited, a smile tugged at the corners of my mouth. A lightness made space in my heart. Peace was present. I sensed the nearness of the Lord. I called his name again, Lord, Jesus. My smile deepened. I have been calling on him ever since.

The Uniqueness of the Lord's Name

It would be hard to imagine a name more loved worldwide than the name of Jesus Christ. Millions around the world love the name of the Lord. Many suffer severe persecution and even death rather than disown it. At the same time, there is not a name more maligned. Millions use the name of Jesus as a daily curse without giving it a second thought. There's no counting how many times the Lord's name is uttered in frustration and anger when things go poorly.

Why is this? It would make more sense when something awful happens to curse the name of some mass murderer like Hitler or Stalin or the name of Satan, the ultimate hater of mankind. But that isn't the way it works. Here's what Jesus did to have his name treated with such disdain: He revealed a loving God to mankind, stood up for outcasts, healed the sick, manufactured food, walked across a wind-tossed lake, gave hope to the hopeless, and ultimately sacrificed his own life for the sake of others. Those are all reasons for honor, not disdain. The primary explanation is that God's enemy, whose lying influence permeates this present age, wants this name to be dishonored and trivialized above all others. But in God's eternal plan, the age-long effort to ridicule, stain, and shun the name of the Lord Jesus will fail.

What is your experience with the name of the Lord? Is it a place of retreat where you find strength, solace, and security as Solomon described in Proverbs 18:10, "The name of the Lord is a strong tower, the righteous runs into it and is safe." If so, you are truly blessed.

If your experience with the name of the Lord is less than that, or if you have the sense that there are depths to the Lord's name that you have not yet discovered, then this was written with you in mind. It was written to bring you into a deeper relationship with your Lord and to unleash the power of this name into your life. If, for you, "in the name of the Lord" or "in your name" have become meaningless phrases or add-ons put at the end of prayers without thinking about it, there is hidden treasure ahead. Paul offered this amazing invitation to all believers in Colossians: "Whatever you do in word or deed, do all in the name of the Lord Jesus" (Colossians 3:17).

But how do we access those riches?

The Name of our Creator

When you first meet someone, what is the point of introduction? Naturally, it is that person's name. We want people to know our name. This is no different with our creator God, who put a natural desire in our hearts for relationship with him. So let's meet this mighty One.

In Genesis 1:1 in the original Hebrew language, He is introduced to us as Elohim. The Scriptures say this: "In the beginning Elohim created the heavens and the earth..." In this context, the Hebrew word carries this meaning: "one Spirit in plural." Our Elohim, the creator God, is one Spirit, but He is plural. He is Father, He is Son, He is Spirit. Yet, He is One. This is a great mystery, wonderful to consider. That's why Genesis 1:26 reads like this, "Let us make man in our image, after our likeness..." There are 32 references to Elohim in Genesis 1 alone and 2500 uses throughout the Old Testament. How important it is that we realize that the God we call on today is our mighty creator Elohim, one God: Father, Son and Spirit! Because the Hebrew word for Elohim was also used to refer other types of heavenly bodies, our God wanted us to be clear which Elohim is our mighty Creator, the One Spirit in Plural. He wants us to know him personally in contra-distinction to all others. So how does this become personal?

Yahweh, the Special Name of God

When I was young, as part of a church-going family, I was taught the Lord's Prayer. I remember hearing that prayer every Sunday morning for years, recited by our pastors in deep, holy sounding tones, "Our Father, who art in heaven, hallowed be thy Name..." At that point I would think, "God, you may care about me; but you are so far, far away, way out there in heaven somewhere. How could you even find me?" Suffice it to say that my experience with the Lord was not very personal. But that is not how our God meant for things to be.

In the German language there is a formal word for the pronoun "you." The word is Sie. This form of the word is used in business, when meeting people for the first time, or in conversation with those you do not know well. But there is also a personal word for the pronoun "you." The word is Du. When you have become friends with someone or are part of the same family, instead of using the word Sie when talking with them, the word Du would be used.

Our family lived in Germany for several years when our oldest children were young. We will always remember the time it took us to move from a formal relationship with those in our large apartment building to one that was more personal. To do that we joined with them in community activities, informal outings and evenings together. Finally, the day arrived when they hosted a special get-together for us. In that gathering they officially let us know that from then on, we would call each other by Du. We felt honored and warmly welcomed.

In the original Old Testament Hebrew, God is most often called Jehovah or more accurately, YHWH, (pronounced Yahweh). For example, this name was the one revealed to Moses in Exodus 6:2 when God said, "I am the LORD." To use the German analogy, by using the name of Yahweh, our God, Elohim, moved from Sie to Du with us. What is fascinating is that the Scriptures call God by this name, Yahweh, over 6800 times in the Old Testament. That is more than double the use of Elohim. What is truly meaningful is that Yahweh is the most personal name used to refer to God. When the Lord introduced himself to Moses in this way, he was showing that he wanted Moses to know him personally, even intimately. The use of this name, which means I AM, shows us how personal and present God wanted to be with his people. He was not the God who would be something great to them someday or who was something great to them in the past. No, he is the God who is, the God of the present, the God who is with us now. As Elohim, He is our Creator God, the all-inclusive Trinity, and as Yahweh He is our intimate Lord. In all this our God wants us to know that we are warmly welcomed, indeed, earnestly desired, in his presence.

The Psalms Show Us the Way

The following examples in Psalms make clear how the Old Testament believers used the name of Yahweh to contact him. There are over a hundred references in the Psalms to the use of the Lord's name. Here are a few of them that use the Hebrew forms of his name.

Psalm 4:
1. Answer me when I call, O Elohim of my righteousness!
You have relieved me in my distress;
2. Be gracious to me and hear my prayer.
3 But know that Yahweh has set apart the goodhearted man for Himself; Yahweh hears when I call to Him.

Psalm 18: A psalm of David who spoke to Yahweh the words of this song on the day Yahweh rescued him from the hand of his enemies and from the hand of Saul. He said:
1 "I love You, O Yahweh, my strength."
2 Yahweh is my rock and my fortress and my deliverer,
My Elohim, my rock, in whom I take refuge;
My shield and the horn of my salvation, my stronghold.
3 I call upon Yahweh, who is worthy to be praised,
And I am saved from my enemies.
4 The cords of death encompassed me,
And the torrents of decadence terrified me.
5 The cords of Sheol surrounded me;
The snares of death confronted me.
6 In my distress I called upon Yahweh,
And cried to my Elohim for help;
He heard my voice out of His temple,
And my cry for help before Him came into His ears.

Psalm 5:11-12 makes a beautiful connection between loving the name of the Lord and enjoying his presence:
11. "But let all who take refuge in you be glad;

Let them ever sing for joy.
Spread your protection over them,
that those who love your name may rejoice in you.

12. For surely, O Yahweh, you bless the righteous; you surround them with your favor as a shield."

Moving into the New Testament

Jesus' introduction to this planet came in a mighty way with yet another name signifying his presence. It was made by no less than the angel messenger Gabriel. Listen to Gabriel's announcement of Jesus' coming: "Do not be afraid, Mary, for you have found favor with Elohim! And behold, you will conceive in your womb and bear a son, and you shall name him Y'Shua. He will be great and will be called the Son of the Most High, and Master Yahweh, your Elohim, will give him the throne of his father David, and he will reign over the house of Jacob forever and his kingdom." (Luke 1:26-38)

Here was Yahweh, come in the flesh, to provide salvation for all. This was history-making. All heaven was paying attention. Here is Elohim, the creator God, named 32 times in Genesis 1, now becoming incarnate on the earth as "I AM is Salvation."

Can we see it? This name Y'shua is a powerful one, indeed the most powerful in all the Universe. In its Hebrew meaning it combines the name of Yahweh and the word for salvation. Thus it meant Yahweh (the personal God, the present God, the I AM) is salvation.

There was only one Y'Shua. There was no one else who had ever claimed to be the I AM, come in person as salvation. In the religious first-century world of the scribes and Pharisees, this name alone marked Jesus for death.

The Scriptures plainly show us the power of this name. John 1:12 shouts it out: "As many as received him (Y'shua), to them he gave the right to become children of Elohim, even to those who believe in his name." That name brought with it the presence of the Father God, the One who would bring salvation to the earth. Jesus declared it: "I have come in my Father's name." Jesus had come in the name of the Father, bringing the presence and rule of his Father to earth. Sadly, most of the people could not see it and did not receive him.

Throughout his time on Earth, Jesus said things that made the religious leaders want to kill him. Those things, not the least of which was boldly representing his Father's name, led to his death. Indeed, the Lord's enemy was totally opposed to the authority of Jesus. He didn't want a man on the earth acting in the name of the Lord and showing forth the attributes of the living God. He knew that under such conditions, his power was broken. The enemy did not want this name exalted then. He does not want it exalted now.

But the Lord Jesus is determined that we will know his Father. He is determined that through His Name we will be brought into the presence of his Father God. Jesus knew that on the other side of his death was his glorious resurrection. Then the power of Jesus' name manifested through the resurrection life of Jesus in his followers would become widespread!

Thomas Has a Revelation

The disciple Thomas has always received criticism for his doubting, for his needing to see the Lord for himself and feel his wounds before he would believe. Unfairly, he has become known as "doubting Thomas." That's pretty harsh for a man who faithfully followed Jesus around for three years but just happened to miss one of the greatest meetings of all time. When he heard about Jesus' glorious post-resurrection appearance in the midst of the disciples and the blowing of the Spirit into the disciples, it's no wonder that he felt disappointed and skeptical. He wanted to see for himself.

Notice that Thomas did not go anywhere. He did not stop hanging out with the other believers. He didn't get depressed and leave. No, there he was with them eight days later when Jesus showed up again. Jesus immediately reached out to Thomas and told him to touch his scarred hands and side and believe again!

Thomas' reaction is one of mighty revelation. He truly realizes who this mighty One is who stands in front of him. Consider his amazing words of faith, "You are my Master and you are my Elohim!"

Thomas gets it. The mighty Elohim, the One Spirit in Plural, is standing in front of him as the glorified Lord Jesus, able to penetrate the hearts of men and come and live in them. This is our great Savior; this is our great God.

And what is the Lord's response? Jesus affirms Thomas' words, "Now that you have seen me you have believed. Blessed are those who do not see me and believe." That's us! You and me! We are those who believe that our Father God has come in his Son and that they have the power to give themselves to us through the Spirit. These are mysterious and magnificent truths, now to be enjoyed through the Name that is above every name. Remember these words taken from John 1:12: "But to those who did receive him, he gave the authority to become the sons of Elohim, those who have believed in his name."

Calling on the Lord, A New Day Has Begun

What was the response of Jesus making his name available to those who believed in him? They began to call on him. This rejoices the heart of God. What do new parents want to hear first from their infant children? Is it not the name that they want to be called? "Did you hear that?" yells Mommy or Daddy when their little one says their name for the first time. "She said my name," or "He knows who I am!" Parents know the excitement of that experience. Our Lord feels the same joy when, in response to his offer of salvation to us, we begin to call on him by name. The Scriptures validate this.

Listen to how Paul opened his letter to the Corinthians: "Paul...to the church of God which is at Corinth, to those that have been sanctified in Christ Jesus, saints by calling, with all who in every place call upon the name of our Lord Jesus Christ, their Lord and ours." These verses show that Paul had previously taught the believers in all the churches to call on the Lord; to have his name, "Lord Jesus," on their lips. Why would he do that? Because, as Peter preached in Jerusalem, "There is salvation in no one else for there is no other name under heaven that has been given among men by which we must be saved." Imagine the sisters and brothers in Ephesus hearing these truths. They, who were forced to call

Caesar as Lord, were finding out there was a greater Lord, the Lord Jesus. By calling on His name they could find peace and life.

It's no wonder that God's enemy wanted the name of Jesus to be disdained and trivialized. Why is God's enemy so set against this name? The reason is clear: the power of salvation is available in Jesus, the person who has this name.

Forty days after the resurrected Jesus ascended into the heavens, Peter declared to a vast crowd in Jerusalem, "And it shall be that everyone who calls on the name of the Lord shall be saved." How does that work? When we first invite the Lord to come and dwell in us, his presence makes our spirit alive to God. When we subsequently call on him, we come in contact with that spirit, where Christ, the deliverer of our salvation, now resides.

Paul further helped us understand how we access this life when he wrote the following to the church in Corinth: "Therefore I make known to you that no one speaking by the Spirit of God says, 'Jesus is accursed,' and no one can say 'Jesus is Lord' except by the Holy Spirit" (1 Corinthians 12:3). Just like the Corinthians and the Ephesians, we can access the riches and salvation found in spiritual realms by confessing the Lordship of Jesus. Paul said the same thing to the Romans when he wrote, "The word is near you, in your mouth, and in your heart: that is, the word of faith, which we are preaching, that if you confess with your mouth Jesus, Lord and believe in your heart that God raised him from the dead, you shall be saved; for with the heart man believes, resulting in righteousness; and with the mouth he confesses, resulting in salvation… for the same Lord is Lord of all abounding in riches for all that call upon him, for whoever will call on the name of the Lord will be saved" (Romans 10:8-12).

The Lord himself helps us in this practice. Look at these words of Paul to the Galatians, "Because you are sons, God has sent the spirit of his Son into our hearts crying, Abba, Father." (Galatians 4:6) By turning to the Lord in our spirits, we can join in with this calling on our Father. We can come to our eternal Father because he has given us his name.

The good news is we can come to the Lord with whatever is going on in our lives. Whether we are up or down or doing well or doing poorly, he wants us in his presence. Today we have the shed blood of

Jesus to cover any shortcomings that we may have and to give us entrance into the Father's loving presence.

But there is a battle involved in taking up the Lord's name. Those who make up the body of Christ have been called out of darkness to make his name known. This is what Peter did in Acts 2:38, where we read, "Then Peter said unto them, Repent, and let each of you be baptized in the name of Jesus Christ for the forgiveness of sins, and you shall receive the gift of the Holy Spirit." We see Peter in action again in Acts 3:6: "But Peter said, 'I do not possess silver and gold, but what I do have I give to you: In the name of Jesus Christ the Nazarene—walk'" and in Acts 4:12 where he declared, "And there is salvation in no one else: for there is no other name under heaven that has been given among men, by which we must be saved." There is power and purpose in this great name. Peter knew it. Paul knew it. Now it's our turn to discover what they knew to be true: there are spiritual blessings waiting for us in learning to call on the name of the Lord. Confessing his name, and putting ourselves under his Lordship, opens those blessings to us. This is not some type of mantra or a nervous placing of the word "Lord" in every other word of our prayers, but a sincere turning to the one who is greater than we are and allowing him access to our life.

God's Enemy Opposes this Name

The authorities responded to Peter the same way they did to Jesus. They warned the disciples not to speak any longer in this name. Here is what they said: "And when they had summoned them, they commanded them not to speak or teach at all in the name of Jesus. But Peter and John answered and said to them, 'Whether it is right in the sight of God to give heed to you rather than to God, you be the judge; for we cannot stop speaking about what we have seen and heard'" (Acts 4:18).

The disciples knew that it was in the name of Jesus that their strength and testimony lay. They were totally enthralled with Jesus and could not help but speak of him to anyone who would listen. The fact that they had been made a part of his family and given his name was real. They had to spread this incredible news.

When they were released, they immediately went back to proclaiming the excellencies of his name no matter the consequences. They were taken into custody again, and this time the authorities wanted to kill them. But a Pharisee named Gamaliel intervened on their behalf. Acts 5:40 records what happened: "And they took his [Gamaliel's] advice: and after calling the apostles in, they flogged them and ordered them to speak no more in the name of Jesus, and then they released them."

The disciples responded by counting it an honor to suffer for his name. "So they went on their way from the presence of the Council, rejoicing that they had been considered worthy to suffer shame for his name. And every day, in the temple and from house to house, they kept right on teaching and preaching Jesus as the Christ" (Acts 5:41-42). For first century believers, speaking forth the name of Jesus meant declaring to their local rulers that Christ was alive, that he was the one who saved them from the present evil age, and that he had invited them to partake of the riches found in his name. We have the same opportunity today. Perhaps doing so will earn you the disfavor or scorn of those around you. If you are being persecuted for lifting up the name of Jesus, take heart! You are not alone. You are in a long line of faithful witnesses who have suffered to magnify the name of Jesus.

The Name Above All Names

In what name do we trust? Are we looking to ourselves for sufficiency and success, or have we found that there is a name that is above every name that we can turn to? It is a blessed day when we discover that the name of Jesus is the entry way into a whole new realm of living. In fact, there is no real life outside of Jesus. As the apostle John wrote in John 20:31, "…these things have been written that you may believe that Jesus is the Christ, the Son of God; and that believing you may have life in his name."

Matthew 28:18 gives more insight into the importance of the Lord's name: "Jesus spoke to them, saying, 'All authority has been given to me in heaven and on earth. Go therefore and make disciples of all the nations, baptizing them in the name of the Father and the Son and the

Holy Spirit, teaching them to observe all that I commanded you; and lo, I am with you always, even to the end of the age.'" The word "baptized" here means being placed or immersed into. Through faith in Christ we are baptized (placed) into the name of Elohim, the One Spirit in plural, the Father, Son and Spirit. From the Lord's perspective that means we are immersed in all that the Father is, all that the Son is and all that the Spirit is. All the attributes of the One who bears that great name are available to us. Christ becomes our residence, our strength, our place of refuge. We, in turn become the dwelling place of our Lord. Best of all, he is with us always, even until the end of the age. His presence makes all things possible.

The Helper Comes in Jesus' Name

How can these truths be turned into practical reality in our lives? Jesus told his disciples, "These things I have spoken to you while abiding with you. But the Helper, the Holy Spirit, whom the Father will send in my name, he will teach you all things, and bring to your remembrance all that I said to you. Peace I leave with you; my peace I give to you; not as the world gives do I give to you. Do not let your heart be troubled, nor let it be fearful. You heard that I said to you, 'I go away, and I will come to you'" (John 14:25-28). The Lord wants us to be at peace. You do not have to worry about how the Lord will work this out in your life. Jesus comes to you as Spirit to make the blessings of his great name available to you. As you turn to him, he will teach you how to live in his presence. He will make known to you the wonder of who he is. He is the author and perfecter of your faith.

In his prayer to his Father before going to the cross, Jesus prayed, "I have manifested your name to the men whom you gave me out of the world; they were yours and you gave them to me, and they have kept your word...I am no longer in the world; and yet they themselves are in the world, and I come to you. Holy Father, keep them in your name, the name which you have given me, that they may be one even as we are...O righteous Father, although the world has not known you, yet I have known you; and these have known that you sent me; and I have made your name known to them, and will make it known, so that the love with which you loved me may be in them, and I in them" (John 17:6, 11, 25-26).

These words reveal what our Father God really had in mind when he spoke of the place where his name would dwell back in the Old Testament. His true desire was not for his people to come to an earthly city or temple to worship him. He wanted his people to be his temple with his name in and on them. It will take an eternity to fully understand what this all means.

Jesus shows us that to manifest the Father's name means to show what he is really like. He asked his Father that we would be kept in his name—held tight in his loving presence. Consider that the disciples watched Jesus and his comfort level with the Father. To live in the Father's name for Jesus was comfortable, accessible, peaceful. Being in the Father's presence did not make Jesus religious or uptight. On the contrary, it filled him with joy and love. He knew him as his mighty creator, Elohim and his intimate Father, Yahweh. This same experience can be ours as well through the Spirit.

If it is not your practice to encounter the Lord Jesus by calling on his name, why not start today? You can whisper his name or you can shout it. You can groan it, sigh it, sing it or speak it. You can speak it in your heart. You can call out to him while driving in your car, sitting at your desk, standing at the stove, or finishing this sentence. Join the company of believers who throughout the ages have been taking advantage of being on a first-name basis with the King of Kings and Lord of Lords. They have called on him in times of trouble and in times of rejoicing. They have called on him at work and at play, at school and in battle. They have called on him alone and in the company of others.

The results of spending time with the Lord, allowing him to saturate you from within with his presence, are oneness and love. Imagine being loved by the Father the way that he loves Jesus Christ. You are. Imagine experiencing the same degree of unity with your believing brothers and sisters that the Father shares with the Son and the Spirit. That is God's goal for us. He is our Elohim.

God's amazing plan for you and me begins with getting to know him. When you sense a need for the Lord, call on him. He has placed that longing in your heart. The Lord is committed to making the greatness of God known to you.

As the Psalmist wrote so long ago, "The Lord is near to all who call upon him, to all who call upon him in truth" (Psalm 145:18). You can call to your Lord Jesus. You can call on him as your Father, your Papa. You can call on him as the Spirit. He has given us many ways to approach him. The Lord is near to you now. Say his name. Let his name wash over you. Let his name warm your heart and fill you with the joy and closeness found in his presence. For where his name is, his presence is also. He will hear your call.

Heaven, the Realm of God's Presence

"Blessed be the God and Father of our Lord Jesus Christ, who blesses us with every spiritual blessing in the heavenlies in Christ" Ephesians 1:3

What if I invited you to go to heaven with me?

"Wait," I can hear you saying, "I'm not ready to die."

Nonetheless, I invite you to come with me to this amazing place. Yes, it will be an eye-opening journey. Be forewarned; when I speak of heaven, I am talking about one of the most misunderstood words in our Christian treasure trove. There are over 700 references to "heaven" in the Bible. This is a place that is very important to God. In the Scriptures the word "heaven" is generally written in the plural and should be translated the heavens or the heavenlies. For example, "Our Father, who is in heaven" should be translated, "Our Father who is in the heavens." This distinction is important. It helps us realize that this invisible realm called the heavens is not simply a futuristic place where believers go when they die, but it is God's current location, the nearby invisible realm where he is found, where he reigns and to which we have access.

Many different images come to mind when considering the heavenly realm. Some envision it as a place where angels sit around with harps playing soothing music. Others view it as an eternal worship service. Many envision it as a place where large mansions await the faithful who stroll down broad golden streets. Some may be afraid that an endless life in heaven will be boring.

In reality, the heavens are far more than what these images present. The heavens are the realm of God's presence, power and authority, a realm created by him for his habitation. God created the heavens as a place where he would dwell, and reign and welcomes us. But the heavens are not just the place where God lives. We, too, have been seated there in the Lord Jesus. Hear Paul in Ephesians 2:6, "God raised us up with Christ and seated us with him in the heavenly places." That makes the heavens available to us.

Is Heaven Far Away?

How far away then, are the heavens? As a young boy I remember hearing prayers started out in deep, religious tones, "Our Father who art in heaven," or "Our heavenly Father." These opening words made it seem as though the heavens were millions of miles from where I was. I knew God was in heaven and I hoped he was listening. But he seemed very far away, somewhere above all the stars and the planets.

Though I would never admit it, I wondered how a God who was so far away could really get to where I was. I wondered how he could even hear what I was saying. The idea that the heavens are way, way out there is mistaken. Nor is God way out there, either. Such thinking puts a far greater distance between God and his creation than actually exists. "Way out there" is not very accessible. But that's not the case, because God went to great lengths to be here, totally accessible to us.

Consider how close he was to Jacob in Genesis 28:11-18, "And Jacob...came to a certain place, and spent the night there; he had a dream and behold a ladder was set on the earth with its top reaching to heaven: and the angels of God were ascending and descending on it; And the LORD stood above it, and said, I am the LORD, the God of Abraham your father, and the God of Isaac: the land on which you lie, I will give it to you and to your seed. Your seed shall be like the dust of the earth .... and in your seed shall all the families of the earth be blessed.... Then Jacob awoke from his sleep, and said, surely the LORD is in this place and I didn't know it...how awesome this place is! This is none other than the house of God, and this is the gate of heaven."

Jacob called that place of interaction between God and man, the house of God, the very gate of heaven. What was going on there? God in heaven was interacting with man on earth. God in heaven was making his will known on the earth. The communication originated in God, but the result was practical blessing on the earth.

From this encounter we can see that the house of God is to be the place where earth and heaven are joined. What does this mean to us? It shows that the present reality of the house of God today is the Church, the body of Christ collected together, being led by the Lord Jesus in the heavens. The people of God living by the life of God would be how God in the heavens would impact the earth. The church would be the gateway between the will of God in heaven and the fulfillment of that will on the earth.

If the house of God is the gate between the heavenly realm and earth, then that realm must be nearer than we think. Many verses in Matthew make the gap between heaven and earth razor thin. In Matthew 3:2 John the Baptizer said, "Repent for the kingdom of the heavens has come near."

Matthew 3:16-17 says this, "After being baptized, Jesus came up immediately from the water: and the heavens were opened and he saw the Spirit of God descending as a dove, and lighting on him and behold a voice out of the heavens said, This is my beloved Son, in whom I am well pleased."

In chapter 4:17 we read, "From that time Jesus began to preach, and to say, Repent: for the kingdom of the heavens is at hand."

Indeed, the kingdom of the heavens was near, so near that what God said in one realm could be heard by humans in the other. In fact, that realm was so near that they were looking right at it. Jesus Christ embodied the kingdom of the heavens!

Jesus Invites Us to Enter Heavenly Realms

Jesus told his followers in Matthew 5:20 that unless their righteousness exceeded that of the Pharisees, they could not enter the kingdom of heaven. This was discouraging news to the twelve. If that were true, entering heaven would be impossible. The disciples observed the religious leaders' priestly outfits, their austere behavior, and their knowledge of the law. From an outward perspective, these were impressive looking people.

In our day, many have a similar sense when they see a priest, a nun, or someone wearing sacramental robes or other religious garb. Such people are treated with deferential respect in part simply because of the intended symbolism of the way they dress. The first-century Jews viewed the Scribes and the Pharisees the same way. They were the ones who knew the law, who understood and practiced what God wanted. They were thought of as the holy and righteous ones. In the mind of the common man, it wasn't possible to be more righteous than those religious leaders.

But the Lord knew that even the Pharisees were not righteous enough to satisfy the entry requirements for God's kingdom. Not one Pharisee could make it on the basis of his good works. The same holds true today for us. Jesus knew there were none righteous. Entrance into the kingdom of heaven was not a matter of obeying the law or being good or putting on an outward show of piety. Entrance into this kingdom is gained through repentance and faith in Jesus, the one who brought the heavenlies to earth. He is our access to heavenly realms. The ladder that Jacob saw so many centuries ago was a representation of the Lord Jesus. He is the one who connects heaven to earth and earth to heaven. As Paul put it, "through him (Jesus) we have our access in one Spirit to the Father" (Ephesians 2:18). Best of all, for those first century saints, those listening to Jesus' words would not have to wait for years to taste the benefits of that heavenly kingdom.

Jesus Shows Us the Way

Jesus spoke often of the direct connection between man on earth and God the Father in the heavens. There are over twenty references to that connection in the book of Matthew. Consider these verses from Matthew 6:

Verse 1: "Beware of practicing your righteousness before men to be noticed by them. Otherwise you have no reward with your Father who is in the heavens."

Verse 9: "Pray then, in this way, Our Father who is in the heavens, hallowed is your name. Your kingdom come, your will be done on earth, as it is in the heavens."

Verse 26: "Look at the birds of the air…your Father who is in the heavens feeds them. Are you not much better than they?"

Verse 32: "For all these things the Gentiles eagerly seek, for your Father who is in the heavens knows that you need all these things."

Is it odd that Jesus mentioned multiple times in the space of a few minutes where his Father was? If you heard a speaker including such a reminder about his father in the course of a talk, you'd likely think he had a problem. But Jesus did not have a problem. He was making the point that he had been sent by his Father out of another realm called the heavens. That realm was where his Father was. Jesus' home base was that realm. By his example Jesus was instructing his followers that, just as he was connected to his Father in the heavens, they, too, could have access to that same realm and that same Father to direct them.

In Matthew 6:6, when the Lord told his followers how to pray, he said, "But when you pray, go into your inner room and when you have shut your door, pray to your Father who is in secret, and your Father, who sees in secret will reward you." Where might that secret place be? It must be in the heavens because that is God's realm.

When you go into that secret place, God is waiting for you. He wants to reward you with something. And that something is himself. As you fellowship with your Father in heavenly places, he gives you himself. He gives you a sense of peace. He may fill your heart with his love. You may experience a sense of joy in his presence. If you are in despair he may impart the ability to endure the suffering. He could choose to give you a vision of something that is to come. All these are heavenly experiences. Prayer can take us all into the presence of God in his heavenly realm. That's how near this realm is.

Jesus' point is that his Father is in a secret place called the heavens. You can go there. This secret place is the place of fellowship for you and your heavenly Father. The point of connection within us is our heart, our innermost room. When a person receives Christ, that person has a new heart because that is where his spirit dwells. Now your heavenly Father can connect with you there. God builds strength into his people in that secret place. In that secret place you can hear his voice, behold his glory, talk to him, cry out to him, or simply groan before him.

The Heavens and the Church

In Matthew 16:16-19, Jesus revealed the relationship between the realm of the heavens and the church. These well- known verses read as follows:

"And Simon Peter answered and said, you are the Christ, the Son of the living God. Jesus answered and said unto him, Blessed are you, Simon Barjona: because flesh and blood did not reveal this to you, but my Father who is in the heavens. And I also say to you that you are Peter, and upon this rock I will build my church; and the gates of hell shall not overpower it. I will give to you the keys of the kingdom of heaven: and whatever you bind on earth shall have been bound in heaven: and whatsoever you shall loose on earth shall have been loosed in heaven."

Here Jesus showed how the church is built and what the role of the church is. Peter testified that Jesus was the Christ, the son of the living God, a revelation he received from God in the heavens. If Peter had had to wait until the end of time to access the heavenly realm, we still would not know how Jesus would build his church. While some have taken these verses to mean that Jesus would build his church on Peter, a more careful look reveals something greater. Yes, Peter (petros, a small stone) would be an important part of the Lord's building. But the church that Jesus was building would be founded on Christ himself. The Greek literally says, "On this rock, I will build of me the church." The church will be built out of Christ!

Peter himself made this clear when he wrote many years later, "And coming to him (Jesus) as to a living stone which has been rejected by men, but is choice and precious in the sight of God, you also, as living stones, are being built up as a spiritual house for a holy priesthood, to offer up spiritual sacrifices acceptable to God through Jesus Christ. For this is contained in Scripture: Behold, I lay in Zion a choice stone, a precious corner stone, and he who believes in him will not be disappointed. This precious value, then, is for you who believe; but for those who disbelieve, the stone which the builders rejected, this became the very corner stone" (1 Peter 2: 4-7).

So how does that happen from our side? To make the building come to life the Lord gives his people the keys to unlock the door to the realm of the heavens.

What Do We Find Beyond that Door?

That's where our Lord Jesus is seated at the right hand of the Father. That's where believers fellowship with the God who gives real life. The Lord gives to his people the keys to the kingdom of heaven, not the keys to a big vault somewhere loaded with money, or a military base loaded with weapons and ammunition. This is a heavenly kingdom whose presence can be displayed here on earth. Jesus came to earth to release the things that his father had released in heaven.

He watched what his father was doing in the heavens and carried that out on the earth. He listened to what his father was saying and said that on the earth. He set people free and he bound evil spirits. Now, as the body of Christ, we're invited into that work. Jesus taught this when he instructed his followers to pray, "your kingdom come, your will be done, on earth as it is in the heavens."

But what are some of the things God wants released as we ask him to work in our lives? Many think of this in terms of warfare and exercising authority over the powers of darkness. That is certainly a part of the job. My wife once attended a women's meeting in India where most of those former Hindus had at one time in their lives been delivered from demonic possession. There were newcomers there who did not yet know Christ. One exhibited very strange contortions and was under some kind of attack. Thankfully the ladies knew how to pray for her for spiritual release and she became quiet and of sound mind. Calling on the Lord set her free!

For us in our daily walk, how about those attributes of our God that he wants released from his heavenly realm that are needed on a personal basis? For example, Psalms 36 says that God's mercy is in the heavens. We certainly need to see mercy released in our lives and in the lives of those around us. The well-known fruits of the Spirit; love, joy, peace, patience, are all things only truly available to us in the Lord's heavenly presence. Thank God, we have been given the keys to the realm where they can be experienced.

We all need joy, love, and peace. We all need direction or vision about why we are on this planet. These are things that come out of our Creator God, our Elohim. We have been given access to his kingdom, to heaven itself, and to fellowship with our Heavenly Father. There we receive these things from him, bring them to earth, enjoy them and then can give them away to others.

This is the true expression of the body of Christ. It is God's people collectively expressing his heavenly desires and rule on the earth. Part of that includes binding the enemy from meddling in our lives and stopping the advance of the gospel. Part of it involves demonstrating the character and image of God that we find in Jesus Christ. In doing these things, the church will become that which is described in Ephesians 1:23, "The fullness of him who fills all in all." This is the reality of what God showed to Jacob when Jacob saw the messengers of God going into and out of the heavens on that heavenly ladder; the people of God going into his presence through Jesus Christ, accessing heavenly realms and revealing the image of God on the earth.

Our Father's Desire for Us

In Matthew 23:9 the Lord said these words, "Do not call anyone on earth your father, for one is your father, he who is in the heavens."

What does the Lord mean by these striking words? Let's say you were blessed to have an earthly father who loved you deeply. You owe your presence on this planet to him and your mother. Obviously he is a very important person in your life. According to Jesus, should you not honor him as such? Common sense and the witness of your own heart answers yes. It must be that the God who instructed his people to "honor their father and mother" was speaking of something deeper in the passage above.

In this case, the Lord was speaking about our spiritual relationship with him. By referring to the way the Jews regarded their religious leaders, he was casting light on our eternal relationship with God. The Jews were instructed that they should no longer simply accept earthly religious leaders (especially those who represented a legalistic way of relating to God) as their spiritual fathers and hence their source of spiritual life. That source of life was to be God himself.

We should exercise the same caution today. We should not bestow lightly a loving title or familial obedience that rightfully belongs to God himself on religious leaders who may or may not know him. It is the God who is in the heavens who has made us spiritually alive. Our true birth originates in him, in heavenly realms. That doesn't mean we can't have respect and esteem for those who lead us in Christ. Their leadership can be very helpful. We just need to remember that our life source lies in our Father who is in the heavens and honor him as the object of our worship. We do not need to go through any earthly priest to get to him.

Our earthly birth enables us to live in the physical environment of this planet. In the same way, our spiritual birth enables us to live in the heavenly air of God's presence. Our God wants us to know that he has given birth to us. We have a right to enter his heavenly presence. As our Father who is in love with us, he wants to exercise the fullness of that love in our lives. That is of eternal significance. For that, only God gets all the credit.

There is no question about what Jesus considered to be his real place of origin. Over and over he said that he was from the heavens. In John 6:33 he said that he was the bread that had come down from heaven to give life to the world. Those who followed kept saying: "Why does he say he came out of heaven? Isn't he from Nazareth? Isn't he from Bethlehem?" Jesus made it clear. He was from the heavens.

Where are you from? Look at the proper translation of Jesus' words in John 3:3: "Unless a man is born from above, he cannot see the kingdom of the heavens." If you have been born from above, then you, too, can claim a place in the kingdom of the heavens. We have a right to live on earth because we were physically born here. We have a right to live in the heavens because we were spiritually born in Christ. We access that realm through the Holy Spirit.

Because our Father God has placed his life in us through Christ, we have a legitimate right as a citizen of heaven to go to his realm and fellowship with him. That's why Jesus said not to call any man your father, for you have one Father who is in the heavens. He is waiting for you there and you don't have to wait until you die. That's news that can change your life!

The Dream Revisited

Let's return to Jacob's vision of the ladder joining earth and heaven and its practical meaning to us today. In John 1:50-51 Jesus shared some information with his disciple Nathaniel that Jesus could only know through divine means. Nathaniel immediately declared that Jesus was the Son of God and the King of Israel. Jesus replied with this fascinating reference to Jacob, "Because I said to you, I saw you under the fig tree, do you believe? You will see greater things than these. Most assuredly I say to you, you will see the heavens opened and the messengers of God ascending and descending on the Son of Man."

Here Jesus showed that he was the reality of the ladder that Jacob had dreamt about. From Nathaniel's perspective, it was startling news that Jesus knew him before he knew Jesus. Similarly, it is wonderful that Jesus knew us before we knew him. Even knowing who we were, he still died to make us his.

But Jesus was saying, "Yes, that's good news, but listen to this. You're going to see the messengers of God ascending and descending on the Son of Man." Nathaniel was going to see Jesus Christ, the ladder, joining earth and heaven. He would see the glory of God in heaven made available to man on earth. He would see man on earth able to have access to God in heaven. All of that was going to happen through Christ. In miraculous and mysterious ways, God's angelic host (his messengers) would be freed to act on behalf of believers on this planet through Christ. He is the one who joins heaven and earth.

Where does that happen today? Today, that ladder from heaven (Christ) touches earth in the church, the body of Christ. Remember, Jacob said that the spot where the ladder touched earth was the house of God and the gate of heaven. When God's people on the earth join together under the leadership of Christ and allow the rule of heaven to be known on the earth, the reality of Jacob's dream comes into being. To God that is glorious!

Practically speaking, it has always been the Lord's desire that we would learn to fellowship with him in heavenly places. In John 10:9 the Lord said, "My sheep hear my voice and follow me and they will go in and out and find pasture." Go in and out of where? Yes, the heavens, the realm of God's presence. We follow the Lord and he leads us into the heavens to fellowship with him and his Father. We go through Jesus Christ to God; we come out to relate to the world. We go in, we go out. We go in, we go out.

We do that because that's what Jesus Christ did. He went into God for sustenance; he came out to interact with the world. He spoke what he heard his Father saying. He did what he knew the Father wanted him to do. How did he know what his Father was doing? How did he hear his Father's words? He was a frequent and welcome visitor to the heavenlies. In his Father's heavenly presence, Jesus found strength and direction for living in this fallen world. Today, through the Holy Spirit, we can also be frequent and welcome visitors to the heavens.

Christ Died to Make Us Worthy

Will we be as good at it as Jesus? No. While Christ dwells in our hearts, we contend with bodies infected with sin and damaged souls that need renewing. That complete renewal will not be accomplished until Christ is fully revealed. Besides that, we are each single members of his body and, on our own, do not represent his fullness. As such, we function best when we are connected to other believers. But we have his Spirit within us and we will know wonderful moments of experiencing our heavenly place in Christ. Paul put it well when he said, "Not that I have already become perfect but I press on that I may lay hold of that for which I was laid hold of by Jesus…I press on toward the goal for the prize of the upward call of God in Christ Jesus" (Philippians 3: 13, 14). God is calling us upward into his heavenly presence. Let's respond, "Yes, Lord, we accept the invitation."

Despite that offer, some people are afraid to approach God. They are afraid they will receive condemnation; they are afraid they will hear their heavenly Father say, "You've really sinned this time." They've bought into the lie that they are not worthy to spend time with their God. They think they don't belong in his heavenly realm. Their thoughts tell them they can't go in there, at least not right now because God will be mad, disappointed or disgusted with them.

But that is all a lie. Christ died to cleanse us of our sins. Yes, we were guilty, but it is Jesus' righteousness, not our own, which allows us access to God. If you have fallen victim to that guilt dominated kind of thinking, it's time to claim your true inheritance. If you are a human, you qualify to be forgiven by the Lord, enter God's presence and find peace for your weary soul. Then you can come out and share that peace with others. When that happens, we have tasted real church and entered the gate of heaven. We share the food, the richness and the life that is Christ. Again, when we experience that, Jesus says, then we have seen and tasted something that is truly wonderful.

In 2 Corinthians 5:1 the apostle Paul described how this works when he wrote: "For we know that if the earthly tent which is our house is torn down, we have a building from God, a house not made with hands, eternal in the heavens."

Inside of believers there is a building going up. It is a heavenly building, an eternal building. That happens as we fellowship with the Lord, as he builds his life into us. This is our experience in the secret place that Jesus talked about in Matthew 6. God gives us himself when we go to him in the secret place. He works on his eternal building as we fellowship with him. Paul goes on to say in verse 2, "For indeed in this house we groan longing to be clothed with our dwelling from heaven inasmuch as we having put it on will not be found naked…so that what is mortal will be swallowed up by life. Now he who prepared us for this very purpose is God, who gave to us the Spirit as a pledge."

Have you ever groaned because the weight of the world gets so tiresome? Have you ever longed for Jesus to return and make everything whole? That is because there is a heavenly building going on inside you that is longing for the outside to match the inside. Because of Christ's presence within you, you have touched heaven, the realm of our mighty

Elohim's presence. You have tasted the love, peace, joy and fullness that are available to us there. Deep within us we groan for that to become the physical world we live in.

The amazing thing is that we have been prepared for this very purpose. We have been given the Holy Spirit so that we on earth could access heaven and heaven could access us on earth. When we do that as believers, you and I and all those who make up the house of God, the church becomes the gate to the heavenlies. His body becomes the place on earth through which God touches people. His body becomes the place on earth where his image is displayed and where his enemy's influence is destroyed. That is a dynamic, heavenly place to be!

Friends, claim your inheritance. Through the blood of Christ, enter the heavenly place where your Father dwells. Invite him to build into you the riches of that realm. If you haven't before, why not stop right now and invite the Lord to bring the richness of his heavenly presence into your day. Take a few moments to allow him to love you as only our Father in the heavens can. Ask him if you really have the right to touch the heavens now. Then listen for his voice. He will answer that prayer."

The Mystery

**"In all wisdom and insight, he made known
to us the mystery of his will"
Ephesian 1:8-9**

Agatha Christie is the best-selling novelist of all time. Only outsold by the Bible and Shakespeare, this English novelist, who lived from 1890 to 1976, sold over one billion books with another billion translated into other languages. What has made her works so popular over the last 100 years?

She wrote of mystery. Her detective novels captured the imagination of people all around the world. She tapped into a core desire that we all as humans share: to see the mysterious brought forward and then explained.

But where did this deep desire come from? From where does the sense that there is a great mystery that needs solving spring?

This sense comes from God Himself.

Within each of us He has planted a deep awareness that we were made for something special, that we are unique in all creation, that we are part of a story much larger than ourselves. That is because He has written the story and placed a mystery inside it. But what is that story? And what is the mystery hidden in the creation of this universe that once understood, helps our lives make sense? Let's take a deeper look.

God Loves a Mystery

Most people like a good mystery. We enjoy being in on a big secret. There is something in our hearts that is intrigued by the mysterious. We are drawn to it. In its pure form that sense of the mysterious was put there by God, himself.

Every mystery includes a secret, something hidden that keeps the mystery from being openly known. Until we know that secret, we cannot fully solve the mystery.

Many believers are not aware that God had a secret. It was the best kept secret of all time and we are part of it. Yes, you and I were created as part of the greatest mystery the world has ever known. In the most real way, we are part of the revealing of this mystery. In the process, our walk with the Lord becomes closer and our enjoyment of him greater.

The Bible is full of mystery. There is much in its pages that is difficult to understand. Though truth seekers have been poring over its message for thousands of years, different interpretations still come up against one another. Why is that? The Scriptures contain the deep secrets of God. They are designed primarily not to bring us to knowledge but to bring us deep into adventure with God. This adventure includes a great love story. Sadly, however, we often treat God's mystery as a doctrine to be learned or truth to be picked up; simply one teaching among many in our journey through the Bible. We are not encouraged to plumb the depths of the secret that God wove into creation. Because of that we are not alert to God's ongoing creativity and unpredictability. It's time for a change.

Jesus Christ referred to the mystery early in his ministry. He said to his followers, "Unto you it is given to know the mysteries of the kingdom of God: but unto them that are without, all these things are done in parables" (Mark 4:11). There is a mysterious element in understanding God's kingdom. This kingdom is no boring land of rules and regulations where the dull reside. No this is a mysterious realm, the entry into which should be the start of a great adventure story.

Paul referred to the mystery when he sat in a room in Ephesus and wrote to the believers in Corinth. Here is what he said in 1 Corinthians 2:6-10, "But we speak wisdom among those who are mature, a wisdom however not of this age, nor of the rulers of this age who are passing away; but we speak God's wisdom in a mystery, the hidden wisdom, which God predestined before the ages to our glory, which none of the rulers of this age understood, for if they had understood it, they would not have crucified the Lord of glory."

There is much to be taken from this amazing passage. It confirms the fact that there was a mystery hidden in God as he began to create. Amazingly enough, the fulfillment of this mystery results in our glory. While we are surely made to glorify God, we, too, get to share in the glory. That only makes sense for it shows the incredible transforming power of God and the wonderful redemption that the Lord Jesus accomplished for us through his death and resurrection. How that will be accomplished is at the heart of the mystery.

In another of Paul's letters, written to the church in Rome while he was in Corinth, Paul underscored this when he finished up his letter by writing these words, "Now to him who is able to establish you according to my gospel and the preaching of Jesus Christ, according to the revelation of the mystery, which has been kept secret for long ages past but now is made known…according to the command of the eternal God and has been made known to all the nations leading to the obedience of faith."

If we take Paul's words seriously, understanding the mystery is a key ingredient in establishing our faith. And who ordered the mystery to be made known? God did! So let's invite him to show us more about it.

The Mystery and the Rulers of this Age

The I Corinthians passage tells us that there are rulers of this age that did not understand this mystery. Who are the rulers of this age? Consider these words written by the apostle Paul:

Ephesians 3:10: "…so that the manifold wisdom of God might now be made known through the church to the rulers and authorities in the heavenly places."

Ephesians 6:12: "For we wrestle not against flesh and blood, but against the rulers, against the powers, against the world forces of this darkness, against spiritual forces of wickedness in the heavenlies."

Colossians 2:15: "When he [God] had disarmed the rulers and authorities, he made a public display of them having triumphed over them through him [Christ]."

These passages refer to those beings who rule in heavenly places. There is no doubt that the earthly rulers who were in power in the first century did not comprehend the mystery of who Jesus Christ was. But in the bigger picture of God's eternal purpose, Paul was referring here to the spiritual powers, principalities and rulers who were behind those earthly powers. Their ruler, Satan, said to Jesus regarding the kingdoms of this world, "All these will I give you, if you will fall down and worship me" (Matthew 4:9). Satan is the present ruler of this age and, as such, his failure to comprehend God's mystery will result in his ultimate destruction.

The point to remember is that before time began, before there was an earth, a sun, a moon or stars, God had a wonderful, wise and mysterious plan. Before there were rivers, lakes, horses, birds or bushes, God had a secret. Paul said that this mystery, this secret, was so important to God's plan that if the rulers of the age had understood it, they would not have crucified their arch enemy, the Lord of glory.

Why not?

We'll get to that soon.

For now, Paul goes on to say: "…things which eye has not seen, and ear has not heard, which have not entered the heart of man, all that God has prepared for those who love him. For to us God revealed them through the Spirit: for the Spirit searches all things, even the depths of God."

Whatever we can imagine of the great things that God has in store for us does not come close to the reality of what God has planned. That's great news. But is there is a way that we can gain some present time understanding regarding this age-old secret?

Yes.

That understanding comes through revelation by his indwelling Spirit. We can now begin to understand what the rulers of darkness could not.

The Mystery Takes Revelation

Paul elaborated on this mystery when he wrote to the church in Ephesus: "…he made known to us the mystery of his will, according to his kind intention which he purposed in Christ, with a view to a fellowship suitable to the fullness of the times, the summing up of all things in Christ, things in the heavens and things on earth."

God the Father had a secret in mind when he created the earth. God the Son embodied that mystery when he was sent in human form. God the Spirit revealed that secret to his disciples so that they could make it known throughout the world. That mystery includes the gathering together, the heading up of all things in Jesus Christ. Whatever is in the heavens, whatever is on the earth is going to be headed up by Jesus Christ. Is that really going to happen? And, if so, how is the Father going to pull that off?

The servant Christ, the one who laid down his life, becomes the ruler of all things in this universe through his death and resurrection. Because he is the Son of God he has the authority to rule the heavens. Because he conquered death as the Son of Man, he has the authority to rule the earth. The governing of all things will rest on his gracious shoulders. That will definitely come as a surprise to most people who have lived on this planet. Again, this is not an invitation into a life of keeping the rules, predictability and boredom. No! This is an invitation to move from being a reader of an exciting novel, into the very story itself.

But Paul was not done explaining. Here's what he wrote later in the same letter: "By revelation there was made known to me the mystery; as I wrote before in brief. By referring to this you can understand my insight into the mystery of Christ, which in other ages was not made known to the sons of men, as it is now revealed to his holy apostles and prophets in the Spirit; that the Gentiles are fellow heirs, and fellow members of the body and fellow partakers of the promise in Christ Jesus through the gospel…. [T]o me, the very least of all saints, this grace was given, to preach to the Gentiles the unfathomable riches of Christ; and to bring to light what is the fellowship of the mystery, which for ages has been hidden in God, who created all things so that the manifold wisdom of God might now be made known by the church to the rulers and authorities in heavenly places" (Ephesians 3:3-10).

Here was the amazing news. God's plan didn't just involve the Jews. He meant for all the nations to be a part of his inheritance. More than that, he was inviting all who would respond to become part of his own family, flesh of his flesh and spirit of his spirit. But why would that concern you and me?

This plan would become visible in the church, Christ's body on earth. The church cited here is not some lofty building with a tall steeple. This church is a living body made up of all those whom God has called out of the power of his enemy and made part of a new kingdom. The riches of Christ would be shared in fellowship with those called-out ones and so made known to the rulers and authorities in the heavens. If we are part of that church, we are automatically involved.

Paul says that it takes a revelation from God to understand this mystery. I can see why. We are not used to thinking such lofty thoughts about ourselves. But what does it mean to have a revelation? Does it mean we see something about angels and rushing winds and giant horsemen? Not in this case.

Revelation in its simplest form is God showing us what's real. For thousands of years God held on to this secret, waiting for the day when he would reveal it. Think how hard it is to keep a secret for ten minutes, let alone an hour, or a day, or a year. As the American statesman Benjamin Franklin famously said, "Three people can keep a secret as long as two of them are dead." But God is better than that. He held on to the greatest secret ever known for thousands of years until what was called the fullness of time arrived. That time began with the physical, yet divine birth of Jesus and continues to this day.

God wanted the disciples to understand the mysteries of his kingdom. He wanted Paul to understand the secret of his great plan. Now he wants you and me to understand it as well. Notice the emphasis on the words "fellow" and "fellowship" in the passage above. The Gentiles, those who were not originally part of God's chosen people, Israel, were to be fully part of God's people—fellow members of God's family, fellow enjoyers of God's riches and fellow receivers of the promised Christ. These Gentile nations who were considered unclean and hated by the nation of Israel were to become fully one with Jewish believers in the inheritance that God had for his people. Not only that, those nations who were far away from God and without hope in the world were invited to join in the intimate fellowship of the Father and the Son. This was a revolutionary thought in the first century and is still life changing today!

The Mystery Involves Fellowship

This mystery involves fellowship at the deepest level between our Lord and those who put their faith in him. Through that fellowship God shares his incredible wisdom with his body, his church. That's us. As we live out lives of faith, we display that wisdom to the rulers and principalities in heavenly places. Clearly we have an important part to play.

Will God's plan work? Did God know what he was doing in redeeming fallen humans and placing his greatest treasure in them? Eternity will show the answer to be a resounding Yes!

But there's more to learn from Paul on this subject.

In Colossians 1:25-27 we read this: "I was made a minister according to the stewardship from God bestowed on me for your benefit that I might fully carry out the word of God, the mystery, which has been hidden from the ages and generations but has now been manifested to his saints, to whom God willed to make known what is the riches of the glory of this mystery among the nations, which is Christ in you, the hope of glory."

The saints, literally "holy ones," Paul was talking about here are simply those God makes holy by cleansing them with the blood of his Son and putting his Holy Spirit in them. If we are believers in Christ, that means you and me. Holiness in this context doesn't mean practicing perfect behavior. Nor does it mean having sainthood bestowed on you by some church body. No. It means being qualified to enter divine realms, to be able to rest in your heavenly Father's presence, free from sin and condemnation. That's a meaning of holiness that we can all embrace.

To Paul, fully carrying out the word of God included revealing the mystery that Christ, in all his glory, would come to live in his saints (that's us believers). Going farther, through us he would make his glory known to the nations. While those words are difficult to wrap our finite minds around, they definitely point to good things ahead. Please note that the revealing of this mystery contains the full message of God. The secret has now been made plain. We do not need to wait around for the taking of a land or the reconstruction of a temple to begin enjoying the fruits of the mystery. Our focus now should be on accessing the fruits of the mystery in real time. The earth and the heavens are waiting for us to do that. Seeing Christ as he is in us is the doorway to glory.

Paul hammered the point home in the first few verses of Colossians 2: "For I want you to know how great a struggle I had on your behalf... that your hearts may be encouraged, having been knit together in love... as you fully come to understand God's mystery, Christ, in whom are hidden all the treasures of wisdom and knowledge."

Paul is struggling to communicate this great truth: before time began, God had a mystery, a secret which he hid within himself. The mystery would result in our glory and involved both Jew and Gentile. This mystery finds fulfillment through Christ living in us. As a result, we are now on a treasure hunt to mine the riches of the Lord Jesus.

Wait a minute. Are you comparing living the Christian life with going on a treasure hunt?

Yes! And what a treasure hunt it will be.

All the riches of wisdom and knowledge are out there, hidden right within the Lord Jesus. Imagine the wealth! Though the wonder of that truth has largely been lost, it is time to rediscover the treasure that is Jesus in us.

Keep in mind that this mystery is so important, so earth shattering, that if the rulers of this age had understood it, they would not have crucified the Lord Jesus Christ.

So what is the mystery? Clearly we can all repeat Paul's words that the mystery is Christ in us or that the mystery is Christ and the church. But if we say that and then simply go on to the next truth or the next sermon or the next Christian activity, we have not plumbed its depths.

Paul was captivated and motivated by this mystery. This was not something that he learned about in his first six months of being a Christian and then filed away in his memory bank so he could move on to other things. He was called by God to go out and carry the message of this mystery to the nations. He asked the churches of Asia to pray for him that he would boldly proclaim it. He told the Corinthians that he wished to be regarded as its steward. Even in his enduring words to the Ephesians about the intimacy of marriage, he could not help but say that the reality of the marriage relationship was really wrapped up in the mystery of Christ living in union with his people.

That said, if the mystery is so central and deep, how can we better understand it?

The Mystery and Creation

Let's go back and consider creation. By watching how God worked in Genesis 1 we find clues that enlighten us about this mystery that God was hiding in himself. He created the heavens and the earth. Then he introduced light and separated light from darkness. Next he began to build on the visible creation.

As God built, consider his pattern: "And God said, Let the earth bring forth grass, herbs yielding seed, and fruit trees yielding fruit after their kind, with seed in it, upon the earth: and it was so....And the earth brought forth grass, and herb yielding seed after its kind, and the tree yielding fruit, with seed in it, after its kind: and God saw that it was good....And God said, Let the waters teem with swarms of living creatures, and birds that fly above the earth....And God created great whales, and every living creature that moves, which the waters brought forth abundantly, after their kind, and every winged fowl after its kind: and God saw that it was good....And God said, Let the earth bring forth the living creatures after their kind, cattle, and creeping things, and beasts of the earth after their kind: and it was so. And God made the beasts of the earth after their kind and cattle after their kind, and everything that creeps upon the earth after its kind: and God saw that it was good."

Do you see the pattern? There is one significant point made over and over again in the Genesis account. Everything that God created had a common characteristic. Everything contained seed. And, in the most natural of ways, that seed produced its own kind.

That simple fact is tremendously significant. The grass, the bushes, the trees, animals, birds, and beasts—everything produced its own kind. Apples have seed in them that produces more apples. Oranges have seed in them that produces oranges. Monkeys produce monkeys and kangaroos produce kangaroos. This is not rocket science, but it tells us something profound about God's plan for this universe. Remember, in all of this, God had a secret.

Behind the universe that God created was a mystery. But as he created, God left clues as to what that mystery was. God's creation calls out to us every day declaring the simplicity of this mystery. When you see magnificent oak trees, you might be impressed by their grandeur. You may love sitting in their shade. But in the fall of the year, when you look at the ground under them, you see thousands of acorns, all carrying the potential of future grand oaks inside of them. They are all hinting at this mystery. All those oak seeds are trying to tell us the secret. "I came from an oak tree, I will be an oak tree and one day, I will produce oak trees."

Thanks for the science lesson, but what does it have to do with me? Plenty.

There was one significant departure from the creation pattern that makes all this dynamically relevant. Grass produces after its kind, oranges bear the image of oranges, birds produce more birds, cattle look and sound like the cattle that came before them. But look what happened when it came to the creation of man:

Genesis 1:26-27: "And God said, Let us make man in our image, after our likeness: and let them have dominion over the fish of the sea, and over the fowl of the air, and over the cattle, and over all the earth, and over every creeping thing that creeps upon the earth… so God created man in his own image, in the image of God created he him; male and female created he them."

Who is man supposed to look like? What image was man supposed to bear?

Man was to bear the image of God!

That's amazing. The human community, made up of men and women contributing equally, was not to bear the image of man. Men and women, God's highest creation, were to bear God's image and to represent God's likeness on this planet. But that didn't happen. The rulers and the principalities in heavenly places looked down and saw the man that God had created. They saw that this man was given dominion over the earth—earth they considered to be their territory. So, Satan, through the instrument of a serpent, invaded the Garden. He deceived Adam and Eve, and they were tarnished by sin. They lost their dominion over the earth and the possibility of bearing the image of God. But before we go too far in that direction, let's consider what might have been.

Mans' Intended Habitat

When we consider how God designed the creation we can see that everything had an environment where it flourished. Every stage of created life had a realm that it populated and thrived in. Call this planning for success on God's part. The seeds, flowers, bushes and trees were fully at home in the soil. They have been producing there without fail for as long as the planet has existed. The fish found their perfect habitat in the water. To this day the wonders of sea life enchant those who investigate their world. Birds were made to fill the skies above, wondrously picturing for humankind what it must be like to soar above the limitations of earthly cares. All types of beasts are at home on the wide range that we call earth, exerting their dominion according to the power of their life. Everything God's creation needed was available to them to carry out their mandate to be fruitful and multiply.

But how about man?

What was his intended habitat? What realms was he designed to populate?

Surely earth would fall under his domain as the Lord God told him to rule and have dominion over all previously created life. But was there another realm that man was designed to touch? Can it be that God also meant for man to somehow breathe the air of heavenly places? Can it be that God also had in mind for man to feel at home in spiritual realms?

We can confidently answer yes. For only in that way could man hope to bear God's image. Only through access to his creator could man express God's likeness. But how would that happen? Let us not forget that God placed a tree in the middle of the Garden called the Tree of Life. We can safely say that had man eaten of that tree, he would have partaken of a life that was eternal, a life that would have given him access to realms unseen. But, as briefly told above, that was not to be. Man and woman were deceived, ate instead of the Tree of the Knowledge of Good and Evil and as a result were infected by sin. Their loss that day was huge. Besides becoming estranged from one another and setting themselves at odds with the world they were created to rule, they lost their access to heavenly realms. They became earth bound, ever desiring to reach heavenly realms but having literally lost the way.

God Rebuilds

That is why, when you look at humanity around the world today and the civilizations that mankind has produced, you do not see the glory of God. You do not see the image of a glorious, creative, loving and mighty Creator. Instead you see the image of a fallen humanity and the impact of the spiritual forces of darkness who have taken jurisdiction over the planet. That's why God's enemy said to Jesus Christ in the wilderness that all the kingdoms of the world would be his if Jesus would worship that evil one.

The rulers thought that in deceiving Adam they had destroyed God's plan. They knew the man had become sinful and had lost the ability to bear the image of a holy God. But they made a miscalculation, because they did not know about God's mysterious plan. Simply put, they were not in on the secret.

God started working anew, through the Israelites. He drew near to them through the law, the priesthood, the tabernacle and the temple. But all those things only pictured what God really wanted. All of those things were copies of something heavenly that God revealed to Moses on Mount Sinai. God had a secret, not yet ready for revealing.

The Mystery Unfolds in Real Time

Finally, the fullness of time came. Jesus Christ was born in human flesh. Read what John had to say about him starting in John 1:14: "The Word became flesh and dwelt among us and we saw his glory, glory as of the only begotten of the Father, full of grace and truth…. For the law was given through Moses; grace and truth were made real in Jesus Christ. No one has seen God at any time, the only begotten God who is in the bosom of the Father, he has explained him."

At last the one who truly bore the image of God had come to earth. At last all could look and see what God was really like. This one had dominion over the animals. He had dominion over the powers of darkness. He could teach like no one before him. He could turn water into wine and a small lunch into a meal for thousands. He was, in fact, the man Adam was modeled after back in Genesis.

But do we find in any one of those attributes the whole secret? Was the secret that Jesus Christ came to be a great teacher? Did he come primarily to be a great healer? Or was his secret that he was a miracle worker? Or perhaps that he came to be king? No. We can be sure of this because God's enemies knew all these things about Jesus. In fact, because they knew these things, they all the more sought to kill the Lord Jesus. According to Paul, as we have read before, if they had known the real secret, they would not have killed the Lord of Glory. There must be something greater than any of these.

In Cana of Galilee, Jesus went to a wedding. When the hosts ran out of wine, his mother came to tell him about the problem. He replied, "My hour has not yet come." In John chapter 7 his brothers wanted him to go up to the feast in Jerusalem and make a public statement about who he was. Again he responded, "My time has not yet come." Jesus had come to this planet with a specific purpose and timetable in mind. He spoke with authority, he revealed the glory of God, he healed, and he raised people from the dead. His followers wanted to make him king. With their limited view of time and eternity, that was the best that they could hope for. As wonderful as all those things are, the unveiling of Christ as teacher, prophet, healer, miracle worker and earthly king did not fully reveal the mystery of his great purpose.

His enemies thought they did. The prince of darkness, the principalities and rulers of this age and those Pharisees who feared him saw in Jesus a man on the earth they couldn't control. He was the one person on earth over whom they did not have dominion. If you will, Jesus was the one person on the planet who could live in two realms, both earthly and divine. The enemy was in control of the entire planet, so he led Jesus Christ up to a high mountain. He promised Jesus all the kingdoms of earth if Jesus would submit to him. He would give the kingdoms to Jesus if only Jesus would bow down and worship him. But God's enemy was and is a liar. He had no intention of turning anything over to the Lord Jesus.

Here was a man the enemy could not control or deceive. Such an offer might have swayed the rest of mankind, but it did not sway the Lord Jesus. His reply has rung through the ages: "You shall worship the Lord your God and serve him only." Truly, Jesus Christ was a different type of man, a new man. He lived by a life that was divine, the life of God that was in him. As he walked on earth, he revealed the true nature of God to those who had eyes to see. The people wanted to make him king. But Jesus was not looking for an earthly kingdom. God had something greater in mind—something that involves you.

Though the people longed for Jesus to step forward and take control, he refused. His hour had not yet come—the hour when all would be revealed; the hour when God's secret would be displayed. Finally, after three years of revealing God to mankind, Jesus headed for Jerusalem for the great feast of the Passover. Tension filled the air. His followers hailed him as king. His enemies plotted his death.

The Nations Are Added

Events were drawing to a climax. The crucifixion of the Lord Jesus was drawing near. John described what happened next: "Now there were some Greeks among those that were going up to worship at the feast: these then came to Philip and asked him, saying, Sir, we wish to see Jesus. Philip came and told Andrew, Andrew and Philip came and told Jesus. And Jesus answered them, saying, 'The hour has come for the Son of man to be glorified. Truly, truly, I say unto you, except a grain of wheat fall into the ground and dies, it abides alone: but if it dies, it brings forth much fruit. He that loves his life shall lose it; and he that hates his life in this world shall keep it unto life eternal'" (John 12:20-25).

Jesus Christ was about to be crucified. The time of his physical presence on earth was about to end. Up to this point Jesus brought his message to God's chosen people, the Israelites. But then the disciples were approached by non-Jews who wanted to see Jesus, to follow Jesus.

The apostles looked at each other. They weren't sure if that was allowed. They thought the gospel was for them, the chosen people of Israel. Now these outsiders who had no claim to Jesus wanted to see him. The two went to Jesus and told him, "Some from the non-Jewish world are here to see you." As he heard the news, Jesus made this incredible statement: "Now, my hour has come." The Jews knew who he was. Now those from the non-Jewish nations were coming in. The stage was set. Whatever reason the Lord had come for was about to be revealed.

Jesus Christ declared, "Unless a grain of wheat falls into the ground and dies, it abides alone. But if it dies, it bears much fruit." The Lord finally pulled back the curtain. He was a grain of wheat, a seed that would go into the ground and die. Then, rising again, he would produce the fruit of his life in those who would follow him! Jesus Christ is the reality of all that seed that we read about in Genesis 1. He is the seed of God who would produce the image of God in his people. He is the one who would make possible and real God's words, "Let us make man in our image, after our likeness." That was and is the work of Christ. This is the secret of God!

The Mystery Revealed

Finally, we come to the heart of the mystery. Finally, we come to the secret for which Jesus came to earth. He came to be a seed. He came to fall into the ground and die. Then, through his resurrection he would produce much fruit for God.

How was Jesus going to produce that fruit? He would do it as the Holy Spirit. As Spirit, Jesus Christ would be able to indwell his people.

Through the power of his life in them, they could bear his image. They could show to the rulers and authorities the incredible wisdom of God.

Think back to what happened after the crucifixion. Jesus Christ had died. His disciples were gathered in an upper room, not knowing what to do next. The Lord they loved was gone. Then, miraculously, he walked through a closed and locked door into their midst.

Chaos erupted!

Even though he had told them in advance that he would rise again, his physical presence among them was totally unexpected. Thank God, this is how he often shows up in our lives. Though we don't know exactly where to look for him, he finds us. How unpredictable he is! The disciples went crazy!

Jesus cried out, "Be at peace." When they realized it was Jesus, mass jubilation ensued. Their beloved Lord was back. He was alive! Finally, when things had calmed down enough, Jesus said again, "Peace is with you: as the Father has sent me, I also send you." When he had said this, he breathed his own life into them, and said, "Receive the Holy Spirit."

Through his death and resurrection Jesus Christ became the life-giving Spirit. As the Spirit, he could indwell those who believed in him. The Jews had been invited. Now the nations were coming to seek Jesus. Now God revealed his secret plan to put Christ into all who wanted to know him. Jesus, the living seed, would produce the image of God in them. As one body, these believers would express the life of God on the earth. Not only that, in the ages to come they will dwell together, exploring the unfathomable riches that are in Jesus Christ. This is the mystery revealed.

It's time to look at our earth in a new way. Every orange that we eat bears witness to the mystery. Every sunflower loaded with seed gives testimony to God's secret. Jesus, the seed of life, Jesus, the image and fullness of God, is now available to all. Jesus went into the ground to die so that he could get his life into us and fill us with himself. That is the mystery that propelled Paul.

If the rulers of this age had understood the mystery, they would not have crucified the Lord of Glory. Why not? When Jesus Christ walked the dusty roads of Israel, teaching, healing and working miracles, Satan knew that a power greater than he was loose on this planet. His dominions knew that a higher authority had arrived. But they also knew they had everything else under their control. They thought that if they could just get rid of this Jesus, everything would be back to normal. Jesus could only be in one place at a time, whether it was in Cana turning water into wine, in Bethany raising Lazarus, or in Jerusalem proclaiming that a new kingdom was coming. His range was limited. If he could just be killed, then the rulers would be back in control. They thought they had taken care of Jesus on the cross.

But God had a secret.

The Mystery and You

Jesus Christ was crucified and placed into the ground. The enemy thought the problem of Jesus had finally, permanently, been dealt with. But there was one thing those rulers did not understand: The life that was in Jesus was greater than all the forces of death and darkness combined. They did not know that Jesus Christ would come bursting out of that grave. They had no idea that he would ascend to his Father and be wondrously glorified. They had no clue that he was going to return to earth and breathe his spirit life into his disciples.

God's plan from the beginning of time was revealed. The people of God, through Jesus living in them, would now show forth the image of God. As God's people functioned together as a body, sharing the riches of Christ in them, the image and rule of God would be expressed on the earth as the kingdom of God.

The forces of darkness thought they had quenched the source of light and life. Far from it! Now the light spread. No longer was Jesus confined to one physical location. No longer was Satan opposed simply in one town in Galilee.

The rulers and principalities don't just have trouble in Jerusalem anymore. They have trouble in cities across the U.S. in Nepal, in India, in Turkey, across the continent of Africa and wherever you live. Why? Because Jesus Christ lives today wherever his kingdom is found. Wherever his people live under his headship, souls are brought out of darkness, people are saved from lives of meaningless despair and the power of the enemy is broken. The expansion of light, life and love follow in their train.

If Jesus, the seed of Life, is in you, you are part of the revealing of the greatest secret in time and eternity. If not, why not stop now and invite the living Christ to make his home in you through his Holy Spirit? This is the purpose for which you were created.

The mystery is revealed as we know Jesus and become transformed by his life. The greatest gift we can give new believers is to share this revelation with them. The living Jesus, through the Holy Spirit, has actually come to live in them. So begins the greatest adventure we can know in time and eternity. But receiving Jesus is only the beginning. The Lord Jesus comes into us as a seed and patiently works his life into us. Knowing Jesus, sharing the joy we have in him and learning how to live in unity with other believers is God's desire for us. In the ages to come we will be occupied with this same great endeavor, plumbing the depths, the length, the width and the height of the unfathomable riches of Jesus Christ.

This is why Paul told the Corinthians he wanted to be regarded as a steward of the mystery. What greater honor could there be? May God give us ever increasing revelation regarding the greatness of his mystery, Christ in us, the hope of glory...

The Kingdom

"The Father has chosen gladly to give you the Kingdom..." Luke 12:32

What comes to your mind when you hear the phrase "the Kingdom of God"? An image from my youth flashes into my mind of a poorly dressed, somewhat crazy-looking man with a long straggly beard. He's standing on a street corner in downtown San Francisco yelling at the top of his voice for people to repent. He's holding a sign that reads: "The Kingdom of God is at hand."

That was not a good introduction to the Kingdom of God. In fact, it made that Kingdom seem like something to avoid at all costs. God's enemy would love to see that image, or any other negative one of the Kingdom of God, abound. He does not want to see the Kingdom of God made real. Where it thrives, he is defeated.

Of course, such negative images have nothing to do with the real Kingdom of God. This is a place of vitality, beauty, riches, glory, and humility. When the Lord shows us the importance of his Kingdom, it can change the way we live.

The History of the Kingdom

Kingdoms have been a part of life on earth since its creation. In fact, before there was an earth or earthly Kingdoms, there was already a Kingdom. That Kingdom was the Kingdom of God. This Kingdom is also known in the Bible as the Kingdom of the Heavens. Jesus made this plain when he used this phrase 29 times in the Gospel of Matthew. This is the place where God dwells, where he rules. As Psalm 115:3 says, "Our God is in the heavens, he does whatever he pleases." He is the king there! The central feature of this Kingdom is the presence of God Himself. When you have him, you have the Kingdom.

This is a Kingdom where righteousness prevails, where love is abundant, where joy and gladness can be found, where glory shines forth, and where life is expressed with beautiful creativity. This is the Kingdom that Jesus came to earth to establish and grow in those who would follow him. This is the Kingdom that, one day, will fill the universe.

Our First Kingdom Encounter

Kingdom language first appears in the Bible in the opening chapter of Genesis. There God says that he will make a man who will rule on the earth, subdue it, and have dominion over everything that is found there. Listen to the words the Lord spoke to Adam and Eve after he created them: "Be fruitful and multiply and fill the earth and subdue it; and rule over the fish of the sea and the birds of the sky and over every living thing that moves on the earth" (Genesis 1:28). Ruling and subduing are the activities of a Kingdom. But that rule was never rightly established. Man fell through disobedience, and the rule of humankind under God's sovereign will was not established on Earth. Nonetheless, from the beginning it was God's idea that we would be part of his Kingdom.

The Old Testament Plan

The Lord pushed this idea forward when he told the Israelites that they would be a Kingdom of priests to him. This is recorded in Exodus 19:6 when the Lord said to the Hebrews, "You shall be to me a Kingdom of priests and a holy nation." That arrangement was in effect for about 400 years, with justice administered through a system of judges. Eventually the Israelites tired of following a King they could not see. They wanted to be like the other nations around them.

So it was, around 1000 B.C., the Israelites rejected the Lord from being their King. They demanded that he give them an earthly king so they could be like every other nation. In response the Lord spoke to Samuel and said, "Listen to the voice of the people and in regard to all they say to you, for they have not rejected you, but they have rejected me from being King over them" (1 Samuel 8:7). So began the reign of Saul and his successors. While different kings ruled with varying degrees of earthly success and failure, the reality of the Kingdom that God had in mind for his people waited for a future time.

Despite the fact that the Israelites had rejected God as their King, the Lord never relinquished his plan to put his Kingdom in place on the earth. In Isaiah 9, speaking for the Lord, Isaiah wrote, "For a Son will be born to us, a Son will be given to us; And the government shall be on his shoulders; and his name shall be called Wonderful Counselor, Mighty God, Eternal Father, Prince of Peace. There will be no end to the increase of his government or of peace on the throne of David and over his Kingdom, to establish it. The zeal of the Lord of hosts will accomplish this." What a wonderful promise this was of the Kingdom to come!

During this same time period of Isaiah, around 730 B.C., the Lord spoke of similar events through the prophet Micah. In foretelling the coming of John the Baptist as the forerunner of Jesus, these words were recorded: "I will surely assemble all of you, Jacob. I will surely gather the remnant of Israel. I will put them together like sheep in the fold. Like a flock in the midst of its pasture, they will be noisy with men. The breaker goes up before them; they break out, pass through the gate and go out by it. So their King goes out before them and the Lord at their head" (Micah 2:12-13). Seven centuries later, John appeared as the breaker, calling Israel to repentance before the coming of the Lord Jesus, born to be their King.

Through the prophet Jeremiah, about 120 years later, the Lord confirmed his plan: "Behold the days are coming, declares the Lord, when I will raise up for David a righteous branch and he will reign as king and act wisely and do justice and righteousness in the land. In his days Judah will be saved and Israel will dwell securely; and this is his name by which he shall be called, 'The Lord our righteousness'" (Jeremiah 23:5-6).

Praise the Lord, the King is coming!

The Kingdom Comes in Real Time
The View from Earth

The birth of Jesus Christ on this planet was the pivot point on which recorded history and eternity turns. Whether we call the current year C.E. (Common Era) or A.D. (Anno Domini: In the year of our Lord), we are still marking time according to the birth date of Jesus. And, regarding that event, don't be lulled to sleep by sweet songs like "Away in a manger, no crib for his bed, the little Lord Jesus lays down his sweet head." Kingdoms were about to collide in the coming of the Christ. Here is Gabriel's announcement to Mary about the one who would be miraculously born to her, "He will be great and will be called the Son of the Most High and the Lord God will give him the throne of his father David; and he will reign over the house of Jacob forever and his Kingdom will have no end" (Luke 1: 32-33).

Israel had a King at the time. His name was Herod. He was an evil, vindictive, cruel ruler with a long history of oppressing the people under his rule. Nor was he about to turn his Kingdom over to anyone else. But he had no idea that the Lord God, Elohim, the creator of the universe, had been planning this confrontation since time immemorial.

The Amazing Real Story of the Magi

Three men on camels carrying gold, frankincense and myrrh, journey from a long distance to find a baby born in a manger. You've likely heard the story. It's recorded in Matthew 2. This is pretty much what most of us have learned about the Magi and the birth of Jesus. But is this the whole story? Or is there much, much more?

Why, for example, would the arrival of three men on camels have caused Herod and all the chief priests and scribes, and indeed, all of Jerusalem, a city of perhaps 75,000 people, to be troubled as Matthew 2:3 describes? And how did they know about that star? And how did they know it was connected to one coming who would be King of the Jews? There is actually a great history behind the coming of the Wise Men to Jerusalem. This back story shows us the amazing planning our great God did in bringing his Kingdom to this earth.

First of all, consider how many people might have actually been in the entourage from the East. This was likely a 1000-mile journey across what was mostly desert. It would have taken at least a month to make the journey. Soldiers would have been necessary to protect the travelers from marauding bandits. Extra camels and support people would have been needed to carry the food, tents, cooking supplies, water, and everything else needed to travel across the desert. This was the journey of a lifetime for these wise men. No doubt many would have signed up to come. We can only speculate as to the total number of travelers, but it was likely to have been a massive band. Only a large number would have struck fear into the hearts of Herod and all those in Jerusalem.

Who Did the Wise Men Represent?

To add to that, consider the land and history of where the wise men came from. It was called Parthia, at the time, and was the chief rival to Rome for supremacy in the known world. In fact, Rome and Parthia fought wars against each other for control of what is now the Middle East. In 53 B.C., the Parthians delivered one of the greatest defeats the Romans ever suffered in a town called Carrhae in what is today southeast Turkey. Over

40,000 Roman soldiers were killed. In 40 B.C. the Parthians actually conquered the regions that included Jerusalem.

Once Rome had driven the Parthians out, Herod was placed in charge of the region around 39 B.C. He continued to have ongoing skirmishes with the Parthians and was definitely well known to them. One ancient record states that one of Herod's rivals for power, Antigonus, offered the Parthians a large sum of money to kill Herod. So there is history between Herod and the Parthian army. Is this one reason why Herod would have been "troubled" to see a large caravan of travelers accompanied by a cohort of Parthian soldiers approaching Jerusalem in the Spring of 2 or 3 B.C.?

Where Did the Magi Get Their Knowledge?

Now let's consider the Magi themselves. Where did they get their information about the Messiah, King of the Jews? The wisdom gathering of the Magi has its roots in events that took place around 600 years before the birth of Jesus. Young men named Daniel, Shadrach, Meshach, and Abednego, among others, were taken captive by the Babylonian King Nebuchadnezzar in Jerusalem and taken to Babylon. There Daniel had many great adventures. We all know the stories of Daniel and the Lion's Den and the story of the fiery furnace. Then there are the stories of the King's dreams and Daniel's interpretations. Because of these events and his special favor from God, Daniel became the chief wise man in the Babylonian court, serving under such kings as Nebuchadnezzar, Belshazzar, Darius, and Cyrus.

Daniel had a strong heart towards his God, the God of the Hebrews. He shared his faith and knowledge of the one true God with Nebuchadnezzar and all those around him. His stature and wisdom became so great that in the book of Daniel, chapter 2, we read that Nebuchadnezzar elevated Daniel to be the governor of all of Babylon and declared him to be Chief over all the Wise Men in the land. (Daniel 2: 46-48). In other words, Daniel became the Chief Magi of all Babylon.

We can be sure that from that lofty post Daniel began the teaching of the Hebrew Scriptures to all who served under him and came after him.

They also would have known of the current revelations he was getting from the Lord. This included the specific revelation of a King that would be coming to the Jewish nation and the specific time period in which the promised King of the Jews would be born. Those prophecies can be read in the Old Testament book of Daniel.

Down through the centuries, the wise men of Babylon became a type of royal priesthood. It was they who anointed kings and prophesied about events to come. As they continued to hold to the teachings of Daniel, the day finally arrived when one of the prophecies came to reality. As they studied the ancient records, they knew the time was near for the promised King of the Jews to be born. When they saw a special star in the sky, they knew the time was at hand.

Confrontation in Jerusalem

So it was that one fateful day the wise men from the East loaded up their camels and headed west to find the One whose coming had been prophesied almost 600 years earlier. The light from the heavenly star affirmed their route, confirming to these students of both history and the natural world, the spectacular events that were taking place. As the news of their coming reached Jerusalem, Herod was in a panic. Was this another Parthian war party? Why were they here? Herod knew of the power and stature of these wise men. They traveled in royal style. They were clearly men of great purpose.

But they had not come in the name of war. They had come in the name of worship.

Consider their earth-shattering words, "Where is He who has been born King of the Jews? For we have seen his star in the East and have come to worship Him." They were not there to war against Herod. They were not there to conduct some kind of peace treaty. They were there to worship the One who had been born King of the Jews.

Of course Herod was troubled. Of course the religious leaders of the day were worried. They had not been doing their homework. They had not been studying the ancient writings that should have prepared them for the coming of the Messiah. Far from it.

Herod's reaction was sadly predictable. He was intent on holding on to his own power. The same is true of most of those around him. He deceitfully sent the wise men off to learn more of the promised King while plotting how best to eliminate the threat to his own rule.

Joyfully for them, the wise men found the Christ child, the real King of the Jews, in Bethlehem. They laid their gifts at his feet, and rejoiced in his presence. A vision given to their Chief Magi, hundreds of years before, had become reality. The purpose of their lives on earth had been wonderfully realized. They headed home with great joy in their hearts. The role laid out for them by the Eternal God centuries ago had been realized.

A great drama continued as Herod tried to blot out this threat to his throne. A multitude of young boys died when Herod had all the boys under two years of age slaughtered in the Bethlehem region. A great conflict had erupted on earth's shores. A new King had arrived on Earth to claim the hearts of those who would love him. But there would be tremendous opposition, and the Kingdom would not come without cost.

The Kingdom Comes in Real Time: The View from the Heavens

While this was happening on Earth, what was going on in the Heavens? Undoubtedly, there was drama there, as well. As long as there had been a creation, there had been worship of Yahweh Elohim, the Creator God. The Old Testament Hebrews were called over and over in the Psalms to worship the Lord God and to bow before him. His pre-eminence in the universe was clearly made known in the opening commandment given to his people, "I am the Lord your God, you shall have no other gods before me" (Exodus 20: 2-3).

But listen to the mighty declaration made by the Almighty God when Jesus Christ is born on this earth:

"And when He again brings the firstborn into the world, He says, 'and let all the angels (messengers) of God worship him!' And of the angels he says, 'who makes his angels winds and his ministers a flame of fire,' but of the Son he says, 'Your throne, O God, is forever and ever, and the righteous scepter is the scepter of his Kingdom'" (Hebrews 1: 6-8).

This was a mind-boggling development. The creator God, the King of kings, commanded his angels to direct their worship in a new direction – yes, toward Earth, itself. They were now to worship a human, one named Jesus, the Messiah. In the Hebrew language his name was written Y'Shua. This amazing name carried the name of Yahweh along with the Hebrew word for salvation. Here was the great I AM showing up on Earth as salvation. Not only that, he would sit on a throne and rule over an eternal Kingdom.

All heaven was ablaze with excitement. No doubt as the news filtered through unseen heavenly realms, the enemies of God, the powers and principalities of darkness also took notice. Worship a man? Worship someone who has taken up residence inside their domain? Never!

We have already seen the warfare that had broken out on Earth. Can we also see that the heavens were in tumult over these developments? One had been born who was called the King of the Jews. But in the planning of God, he would not only be the King of the Jews but the ruler of all mankind and indeed of all creation, visible and invisible.

The Coming of John the Baptist

When a man named John showed up in the wilderness of Judea announcing the coming of the Messiah, he broadcast that the great invasion of this planet from heavenly realms was underway. John's message was completely Kingdom centered. His words were incredible: "Repent, for the Kingdom of the heavens is at hand" (Matthew 3:2). This is the breaker going before the King that we previously met in Micah 2.

To get a feel for what this meant, imagine how the French must have reacted in June of 1944 when they heard the news that the American-led invasion was underway. This was no idle piece of news to them nor a subject for theological debate. They began immediate preparations to receive them. Why? Because America was a real place with real armies, real weapons, and a real interest in returning freedom to Europe. In a similar way, the heavens are a real place with a real-life force with real designs on this planet. Accordingly, John was letting the people of Israel know that the forces in heavenly realms were about to be set loose on Earth in a new and dynamic way.

Unlike the distress that any announcement about one earthly country invading another would cause for one side or another, the announcement of God's Kingdom was great news. In fact, this was the best news heard on the planet since the way to the Tree of Life was closed back in Genesis 3. Why haven't we responded in that way? Partly because many of us have concentrated on the wrong part of the message.

When most of us hear about repenting, guilty emotions rise to the surface. We are not drawn to the event being announced; instead, we focus on our own guilt and condemnation. This is exactly what happened to me when I heard that bearded man in San Francisco, shouting out, "Repent, for the Kingdom of God is coming." The only visions I got were of leaping flames in a fiery hell waiting specifically for me.

Metanoia, not Paenitentia

But what was the repentance that John was encouraging? The original word, "metanoia," carried the meaning of changing one's mind and purpose as the result of gaining new information. It did not primarily have to do with penitence or fearing an angry God because you were a terrible person. In fact, it was a word used in the Roman military. When a commander wanted his troops to turn around and move in a new direction, the charge would go out, "Metanoia!" Turn and go!

When John exhorted the people to repent, he did so because a new Kingdom was on the way. He was telling them they were going to need a whole new mindset. Life on this planet was about to totally change. They would need to learn how to turn to a new source of life. Did that involve confessing sinful ways of living and turning to God for new life? Yes, but those repenting did not stop there. John was drawing them to a new way of living, inaugurated through Jesus Christ. Humans were about to be offered the divine life of God through Christ. For the first time, humankind would be able to live intimately under God's heavenly kingship. This was fantastic news then and still is today.

Changing One's Mind Becomes Doing Penance

Sadly, over time the meaning of repentance changed. When the Latin Vulgate translation of the Bible was produced around 380 A.D., "metanoia" came to be translated as "paenitentia," which focused on penance or acts of contrition. By the time of Augustine in the early 400's, repentance became synonymous with contrition, confession, and penance.

The experience of too many believers has been pretty much stuck there ever since. Rather than focusing on the glorious message that a new Kingdom has come to Earth, we too often focus on the penance we need to do in order to receive it. That was not the focus of the announcement of the Kingdom. If you are seeking that Kingdom, what awaits is not endless reminders of what a sinner you are but an invitation to live out of the life of Jesus alongside other Kingdom members. Along with that a whole new mindset of who God is and how much he loves us is ours for the taking. Yes, that is good news.

It All Starts with Jesus

The opening verse of Matthew's gospel reads, "The book of the genealogy of Jesus Christ, the son of David, the son of Abraham." First impressions are important. Jesus Christ was introduced as the son of David because David was known as the greatest king of Israel. Throughout Israel's history, the king's throne in Israel was called the throne of David. He was a man after God's own heart. The first thing we find out about Jesus Christ is that he is royalty. Your Lord is a King. Not just a King...the King of Kings.

Secondly, Jesus was described as the son of Abraham. Abraham fathered the nation of Israel. Abraham has a double meaning: He is "the one who crossed over" and the "father of nations." Abraham was the first one to leave the old world behind. He crossed over into the land of Canaan as the father of a new nation in a new land. With Abraham you have the promise of a new land with a new nation in it. In Jesus Christ, God brought in the King of a new Kingdom. But he was not coming alone. He is the beginning of a whole new nation. This is not just religious speak. This is a reality with a real government that makes a real impact on the people who live in it.

In Matthew 2:2 the wise men looking for the baby Jesus asked, "Where is he that is born King of the Jews?" From his very birth, Jesus was called the King of the Jews. When Jesus entered Jerusalem shortly before his crucifixion, the crowds shouted out, "Hosanna: Blessed is the King of Israel that comes in the name of the Lord." When the Lord stood before Pilate, Pilate asked, "Are you a king then? Jesus answered; you say that I am a king. To this end I was born, and for this cause I came into the world, that I should bear witness to the truth." Even in his crucifixion, the truth was told. Though hung in a mocking way, Luke tells us that, "a sign above him read in letters of Greek, and Latin, and Hebrew, this is the King of the Jews…"

The truth is that Jesus is the King of Kings. Jesus was a king in his birth. He was a king in his earthly presence. He was declared King of the Jews in his death and crowned King of Kings for all eternity in his resurrection. How do we know this? These triumphant words from Revelation 19: 13-16 describing the Lord Jesus make it plain, "He is clothed with a robe dipped in blood and his name is called The Word of God…and on his robe and on his thigh he has a name written, "King of Kings and Lord of Lords." Why should we think he would want any other role in our lives?

The Kingdom Is Dangerous

Matthew 4:23 says, "Jesus went about all Galilee, teaching in their synagogues, and preaching the gospel of the Kingdom, and healing all manner of sickness and all manner of disease among the people." The Lord took his life into his hands when he declared the new Kingdom. The people of Israel already had a King when Jesus arrived. They were also under the dominion of the Roman Empire and its Caesar. Calling out "Caesar is Lord" was a common practice throughout the Roman empire. Under the Romans, Herod was ruling as the King over the Jewish people. So for Jesus Christ to come along and be hailed as the King of the Jews had great political ramifications.

It is difficult for Americans to relate to the danger inherent in what Jesus and his followers were doing in declaring the presence of a new Kingdom. It would be like going to Saudi Arabia and announcing there was a new king coming, and you were that king. The palace guards would immediately imprison you, because they already have a king.

When I was a young believer living in Isla Vista, a small college town in California, our church fellowship made a large banner that read, "Jesus Christ is Lord of Isla Vista." We hung it between two flag poles that were about twenty feet in the air. We wanted to make a statement to our community about the Jesus we believed in.

Everyone in that community could see this banner as they went back and forth to the local university. A reaction came quickly. One of our neighbors hung out a sign that read, "Lions eat Christians." Then the local officials passed a law against large signs hanging on flag poles. After a while, when we wouldn't take it down, we were threatened with arrest and jail time. We figured we had made our point and took it down. Interestingly enough, shortly thereafter a local newspaper took a poll to see who really was Lord of Isla Vista. Though none of us in the fellowship participated, Jesus Christ still won. The fact is that the enemy never wants his rule openly threatened by the exaltation of Jesus Christ. Not in the first century, not today.

Nevertheless, Jesus continually advanced the cause of his Kingdom. In Luke 4:43, Jesus said, "I must preach the Kingdom of God to other cities also: for I was sent for this purpose." In Matthew 6:31-33 he said this: "Do not be anxious then, saying, what shall we eat or what shall we drink or with what shall we clothe ourselves? For all these things the Gentiles eagerly seek, for your heavenly Father knows that you need all these things. But seek first his Kingdom and his righteousness and all these things shall be added to you."

For Jesus Christ, the establishment of his Father's Kingdom was central. If he was sent for the purpose of preaching about it, how central must the Kingdom also be in the mind of God!

Matthew 9:35 carries the story further: "And Jesus went about all the cities and villages, teaching in their synagogues, and preaching the gospel of the Kingdom, and healing every sickness and every disease among the people." Here again we see Jesus emphasizing that the Kingdom had come. Then Jesus sent out the twelve and instructed them, "And as you go, preach, saying, the Kingdom of the heavens is at hand" (Matthew 10:7). Their message was to be the same as his.

The Lord was aware that up to the time of his death, he alone manifested the Kingdom of God. He alone lived under the rule of his Father and carried that rule out on Earth. But all that was about to change.

The Lord knew that no one could enter the realm of his Father's presence without the righteousness of God. Through his death, the real Passover would cleanse us through the shed blood of God's Lamb. That would allow cleansed sinners to come to God and receive his life. The way to the tree of life would be open again. This would be accomplished by the sacrifice of the Son. The premier Old Testament picture of that was found in the Passover. But the picture was about to find its reality in Christ.

The Final Old Testament Passover is Observed

During his final meal before his crucifixion, the Lord said this to his friends in Luke 22:15: "I have earnestly desired to eat this Passover with you before I suffer, for I say to you I shall not eat it again until it is fulfilled in the Kingdom of God; and when he had taken a cup and given thanks, he said, take this and share it among yourselves, for I say to you I will not drink of the fruit of the vine from now on until the Kingdom of God comes."

Jesus Christ looked forward to eating this final Passover meal with his followers as he had no other. The Passover was the most well-documented Old Testament ceremony. For a Jew, it represented passing from death to life and marked the celebration of the birth of the nation of Israel. In the Passover God's people were delivered out of Egypt and out of death. Jesus Christ knew this.

He had come out of the Kingdom of the heavens to bring the rule of that Kingdom to Earth. He knew that he was the seed of a new nation. He knew that his death, the real Passover sacrifice, would set mankind free from the penalty of sin and open the realm of the heavens to them. So he sat with his disciples and told them that he had been looking forward to this meal with great anticipation.

He was the real Passover lamb soon to be slain. The next time he broke bread with his disciples the purpose of this Old Testament feast would be fulfilled. His body and blood were the reality of the bread and wine that would make life in the Kingdom available to them. Through his death, resurrection and glorification, his Spirit would be released to come and live in them. This was the promise of John 7: 38 where the Lord declared, "He who believes in me, as the Scripture said, from his innermost being will flow rivers of living water. But this he spoke of the Spirit whom those who believed in him were to receive; but the Spirit was not yet given, because Jesus was not yet glorified."

Of course the disciples handled the Lord's glorious, deep news with typical decorum. They immediately got into a fight over who was going to be the greatest in the coming Kingdom. The fact that they didn't yet have a clue about what he was talking about should give us some comfort. Some truths of God take time to be understood.

But Jesus Christ knew the full meaning of all that had gone before and all that was coming. He was fully aware that through his death the glorious and gracious rule of his Father would be extended to the man God had created. He knew that through that rule the subsequent defeat of the powers of darkness was inevitable. Yes, Jesus eagerly looked forward to this Passover. Though it called for his imminent and excruciating death, Jesus was able to give thanks to his Father that it was at hand. The fulfilling of the Passover meant the realization of the Kingdom in the lives of those who would receive him!

Jesus looked forward to eating this Passover with his followers and friends because it was the last time he would eat it as a picture. This was the last time the bread and wine would be only symbolic. Pictures were on their way out, because the next time he ate it with his friends, it would be fulfilled in the Kingdom of God.

The Lord and his Sisters and Brothers Celebrate

Imagine the Lord's joy following his death and resurrection when he returned to the upper room. He passed through a locked door to once again meet, fellowship, eat and drink with his brothers and sisters. After calming their fears, the glorified Jesus breathed his own Divine life into his disciples. The Lord's words from John 20:21 ring out to us across the centuries, "Peace be with you. As the Father has sent me, I also send you. And when he had said this, he breathed on them and said, Receive the Holy Spirit." In those amazing moments we see the initial expansion of the Kingdom of God. Jesus Christ, by breathing his Spirit into his disciples, was literally putting the access road to the realm of the heavens, the highway that John spoke of, into the hearts of his followers!

They surely didn't understand all that was happening to them at that moment. Jesus Christ understood it, though. Shortly thereafter, when the resurrected Christ sat down with his followers to break bread and drink wine, they no doubt rejoiced that the Kingdom had come in them. Peter referred to this in Acts 10:40 when he wrote, "God raised him up on the third day and granted that he become visible not to all the people but to witnesses who were chosen beforehand by God, to us who ate and drank with him after he arose from the dead." The Lord had come to live in his people. His mission of establishing the Kingdom had begun. The Lord and his friends ate and rejoiced.

What Should the Lord's Supper Look Like?

In light of the above paragraphs, what should the Lord's Supper look like for us? For too many believers, partaking of the Lord's Supper is an exercise of introspection that produces guilt. It is a time of penance, not of anticipation or rejoicing. They often leave the table more aware of their sin than when they arrived. What a shame this is!

This is often due to the use of the passages in 1 Corinthians 11 where the believers there were told to examine themselves and consider what they were doing. For one thing they were getting drunk. For another thing they were ignoring the needs of their brothers and sisters who had less than they. Of course such behavior needs adjustment. So if you are meeting with a group of believers who are getting drunk at the Lord's Table and ignoring one another's needs, then, yes, repent and stop doing that.

If that is not your situation, then use the verses in Luke above and the following Scriptures as your Lord's Supper guide. Remember that the

Old Testament Passover, of which the Lord's Supper was the fulfillment, was the most referred to Hebrew feast of the year. And what marked this great feast?

Celebration!

Consider these verses from the Old Testament:

Exodus 12:14: "Celebrate this day (the Passover) as a feast to the Lord; throughout your generations you are to celebrate it as a permanent ordinance"

Deuteronomy 16:1: "Observe the month of Abib and celebrate the Passover to the Lord your God."

2 Chronicles 35:1: "Then Josiah celebrated the Passover to the Lord in Jerusalem… 17: Thus the Sons of Israel celebrated the Passover at that time, there had not been a Passover celebrated like it in Israel since the days of Samuel."

This is confirmed to us in the New Testament with these words of Paul to the Corinthians: "Clean out the old leaven so that you may be a new loaf…for Christ our Passover is sacrificed. Therefore, let us celebrate the feast…" I Corinthians 5:7-8

Can we see it? The celebration of the Lord's Supper marks the fulfillment of the Passover. This is our independence day. From an American perspective, this is the Christian Fourth of July! This is not a time for guilty reflection on how we have fallen short or whom we may have offended. No! This is a time to celebrate all that Christ has done for us in bringing his Kingdom to Earth and making us part of it. This is a time for rejoicing in our salvation and celebrating the King Himself.

The Kingdom Expands

Following the Lord's resurrection and the glorious fulfillment of the Passover, Kingdom action was central in the Lord's thinking. We see this in Acts 1:3: "To these Jesus also presented himself alive, after his suffering, by many convincing proofs, appearing to them over a period of forty days and speaking of the things concerning the Kingdom of God." They weren't talking about something that was going to come into existence thousands of years later at the end of time. They were talking about its practicality then, in their midst. God's Kingdom had come to earth, and it was not leaving.

The Lord remained with them for forty days, talking to them about what it was going to be like following him in spirit rather than in flesh. He may have talked to them about how to deal with the enemy in prayer, what it would mean to deny their fallen natures, and how to turn away from old habits and live by him. Perhaps he showed them how to use the words of the Psalms to go into the presence of God, how to experience deep worship, and how to share life with each other on a daily basis. He spent that time sharing with them what it would be like as they learned to live in his Kingdom by his Spirit.

Listen to the Lord's words in Matthew 28:18, at the end of those forty days: "All authority has been given to me in the heavens and on earth; go then and make disciples, baptizing them into the Name of the Father and the Son and the Holy Spirit, teaching them to keep all that I am directing you, and lo, I am with you always, even to the end of the age." The Lord Jesus had been given all authority in heaven and on earth. That's Kingdom talk. If you go to the heavens, he is in authority there; if you are on the earth, he is in authority there. Praise God, the Lord Jesus passed this authority on to his followers. And the best news is this: "I am with you, even to the end of time." Jesus is committed to you and me, and he is personally with us in this endeavor. This is not up to us to work out on our own!

Jesus' authority was in the disciples individually through the breathing of his Spirit into them in the upper room. It would soon be on them corporately through the anointing of the Holy Spirit on the day of Pentecost. As they went out into the world sharing the reality of what had happened to them, his Kingdom and rule would soon be spreading throughout Palestine and even to the ends of the earth. His rule would extend to people everywhere who repented and received Jesus Christ. What Jesus could not accomplish in human form, he could now do throughout the inhabited earth by means of his Holy Spirit. What an amazing plan!

What Did Apostles Do?

Why did Jesus call those who were to work with him apostles? In the Roman world, the word apostle carried a military meaning. Apostles were military officers sent out by the Roman government to establish a colony of Rome in newly conquered areas. They carried with them the authority of Rome. The apostles were to bring the rule and culture of Rome wherever they went. Cities that resembled Rome in law and culture were established all over the Roman Empire. If you were in one of them, you felt as if you were in Rome itself.

It is no coincidence that the Lord used this word to describe his emissaries. They were sent to bring the rule and culture of the heavens to Earth. This is what the churches they established were meant to be: outposts of the Kingdom of the heavens on Earth that enjoyed the rule of God and experienced the fellowship found in his Kingdom.

The Aramaic word for apostle used in common speech in first century Palestine is worth noting. That word was schlichim. The word carried the meaning, "emissaries sent to proclaim the Kingdom of God and represent the name of Yahweh and his Messiah." This is exactly what Jesus' followers did.

Philip is a perfect example. Acts 8:12 described this scene in Samaria: "But when they believed Philip preaching the things concerning the Kingdom of God, and the name of Jesus Christ, they were baptized, both men and women." Here is a real apostle in action, proclaiming the Kingdom and exalting the Lord Jesus!

In Acts 19:8, when Paul got to Ephesus, "he went into the synagogue, and spoke boldly for three months, reasoning and persuading them about the Kingdom of God." If Paul spent three months talking about the Kingdom of God in Ephesus, there must be a lot to learn about it. Check out what happened in Rome. There, Paul "stayed two full years in his own rented quarters and was welcoming all who came to him, preaching the Kingdom of God and teaching concerning the Lord Jesus Christ with all openness, unhindered" (Acts 28:30). Do you see the apostle at work? Proclaiming the Kingdom of God and exalting the Lord Jesus Christ. From God's perspective, the two are eternally intertwined.

Widening our Boundaries

Preaching the gospel of the Kingdom is still Jesus' mission today, one that he is carrying out in you and in me. He is our King, the one who brings the Kingdom to bear in our lives. As we submit to him both individually and as communities of faith, the will of God can be expressed on this earth. One day all creation will see Christ's glorious mission completed. As Paul wrote in 1 Corinthians 15:24, "Then comes the end, when he (Jesus) delivers up the Kingdom to God, even the Father; when he has abolished all rule and all authority and power; for he must reign until he has put all enemies under his feet. The last enemy to be abolished is death."

The apostle John reported the onset of that great day in Revelation 12:10, when he wrote, "And I heard a loud voice saying in heaven, now is come salvation, and strength, and the Kingdom of our God, and the power of his Christ: for the accuser of our brethren is cast down, who accuses them before our God day and night."

We have a part in this divine drama. Jesus Christ brought the rule of the heavens into our hearts through his Holy Spirit. By his Spirit he is now building a Kingdom that cannot be shaken by the enemy's accusations and threats; no, not even by death itself. He is building a Kingdom that bears the image of God and carries out the rule of God. This is the corporate man that God had in mind way back in Genesis 1. Let's turn our hearts to the Lord today and invite him to reign in our lives. Let's then ask him to connect us with others who are doing the same. These are the building blocks of Kingdom living. May they be so in our experience.

Closing Thoughts: The Kingdom of Love

What can we expect or hope to encounter as we follow Jesus' words to seek first the Kingdom of God and his righteousness in Matthew 6? It was earlier stated that the hallmark, the defining characteristic of the Kingdom is the presence of the King. And that is true. Where he is, the kingdom is present. So what is God, our Yahweh Elohim, like? Let's focus on perhaps his dominant trait.

He is Love.

My first encounter with this God of Love is etched in my memory. I received the Lord Jesus at a Campus Crusade meeting in the Spring of 1968. Immediately after the meeting, we all jumped into our cars and journeyed back to where we came from. In my case that was a three-hour drive back to Santa Barbara, California. As I sat in the back seat, I was oblivious to all around me. The King had ushered me into his presence and wrapped his arms of love around me.

While there was conversation going on, I was barely aware of it. While there were sights to see, I did not notice them. I was only aware that the God I had vaguely been aware of from childhood was holding me in his love. That three-hour drive seemed to last only minutes. Where did the time go? To this day I cannot say.

This was my introduction to the King. This was my first real taste of what it meant to live in his presence. I can thankfully say that I have had many opportunities over the years to experience that love. And the greatest opportunity still lies ahead when the Kingdom is fully established throughout the universe.

I have had the blessing of traveling to many parts of the world. I have met believers of many tribes, tongues, nations, and theological persuasions. Amazingly, there is always an instant bond between us. What is that bond? It is the love of God that has been poured out in our hearts through the Holy Spirit who dwells within us (Romans 5:5).

Consider these wonderful words from the prophet Isaiah, "In love a throne will be established; in faithfulness a man will sit on it, one from the house of David; one who in judging seeks justice and speeds the cause of righteousness" (Isaiah 16:5). It has always been our Father's desire to establish his Kingdom of love with Jesus Christ, the King, at its center. He is the one who makes us righteous through his shed blood.

Jesus closed his wonderful prayer to the Father in John 17:26 with these words, "And I have made your Name known to them and will make it known, so that the love with which you loved me may be in them and I in them." What amazing words, and what an amazing promise! As we live in the Kingdom of God under the rule of our Savior sharing life together with our brothers and sisters, the richness of Divine love can become our own personal experience...

Jesus our Life

The Well Spring of the Kingdom of God
"I am come that they might have life…" John 10:10

"Dad, what's it all about? Why are we here?" my 16-year-old son suddenly asked as we drove down a Sacramento street. I caught my breath. How do you craft an instant answer to the eternal question of the universe; especially one that will make sense to a teenager?

How would you have answered those questions? What is it all about? Why are we here? Have they been satisfactorily answered in your mind?

At the risk of oversimplifying this central issue, let me suggest that the answer to those profound questions is tied directly to an uncomplicated yet profound word…Life.

We are here for Life.

But what do I mean by that? Most believers in Jesus are very familiar with his words in John 10:10, "I have come that they might have life." Jesus tells his followers that he has come that we might have life and have that life in abundance. The apostle John reinforced this same point when he wrote, "These things have been written so that you may believe that Jesus is the Christ, the Son of God; and that believing you may have life in his name" (John 20:30-31).

Yes, God wants to give us life.

If we are not careful, however, we can overlook the tremendous depth of this truth. Or, worse still, its meaning can be unrelated to our earthly experience or relegated to a distant time of future importance.

For example, we may think of the life referred to in John 10 as a quality of life. The Christian life may have been presented to us as a happy life, a life where our sins are forgiven, our basic needs are met, God is on our side and we are on our way to live forever in heaven. Or we may think of it as a life that we will experience in the future, in Heaven with Jesus, when everything will be made new.

What Kind of Life Does Jesus Want for Me?

So what's wrong with thinking this way? Those concepts are not bad. They are simply not adequate in describing the Life that Jesus was talking about. We were created for more than trying to have a happy life on this planet or receiving one when we get to Heaven.

In your efforts to be a good person you may have worked hard to build a peaceful and secure life. Even so, you may be one of the great number of people who have the nagging feeling that God is not very happy with you, that you are not really a very good Christian.

Why would you feel that way? The reality is you're probably not. There are times when Bible reading becomes a chore; your church fellowship becomes routine; your relationship with Christ becomes distant; your relationships with the people around you seem shallow. And then there is the issue of sin. You're aware all too often that you are not perfect.

In addition, life has dealt you some major setbacks. Even though you want to follow Christ, you experience disappointment and disillusionment. At times you feel defeated, thinking that you have let the Lord down, or that he has let you down. Somewhere along the way you watched believers in Christ say and do awful things toward one another, maybe even toward you. If you have been married for a while, you have likely faced disappointment in how you have treated your spouse or kids or how they have treated you. Maybe your job has thrown you for a real loop. Through all of that your commitment to live the "Christian life" has taken a big hit.

If you can relate to any of the above, take heart. There is a richer experience of life available in Jesus. The fact is that the life God wishes us to have is far different than outwardly looking like you or your brothers and sisters in Christ have it all together. It's time to restore the deeper meaning and experience that Jesus is offering us.

The Gospel of John reveals what God has in mind. There we learn that Jesus Christ was unique in the entire universe because, "In him was life and the life was the light of men" (John 1:4).

Jesus Had Divine Life

With that statement in mind, let's look again at the question before us: if Jesus said he had come to give us Life, what was he talking about? While we may assume that everyone breathing has life, John was talking about a totally different kind of life. He was referring to divine life, the life of God, himself.

There was and is a type of life in Jesus that was different than the life that was in anybody else. In Christ was the divine, supernatural, Spirit life of God the Father. In the light that emanated from that life, the darkness of all mankind became evident.

Consider the best-known Bible verse in the world, "For God so loved the world that he gave his only begotten son, that whoever believes in him should not perish but have eternal life" (John 3:16). When it comes to this verse, believers have often been taught to think, "Okay, that means I believe in Jesus, he forgives my sins and when I die, I'm going to go to heaven. When I get there, I'll live forever in a big mansion on a street of gold." While that may be the perspective of many, God was thinking in a different direction.

What the Lord was talking about is the life that is in him, the type of life that he has. Jesus walked on planet Earth exhibiting incredible wisdom, authority, power and love. How did he do that? This is the secret of Jesus. In him there is a heavenly life. It's divine life. It's the life of his Father, God.

The Scriptures tell us, "As Moses lifted up the serpent in the wilderness, so must the Son of Man be lifted up, that whoever believes in him may have eternal life" (John 3:13). The bronze serpent that Moses lifted up was a symbol of Satan being judged and defeated so that we could be free from our sin and old life. When Jesus was lifted up on the cross our sin was placed on him and he took our judgment. That is where the Lord Jesus broke the hold of God's enemy over us. But this isn't just about forgiveness, as wonderful as that is. Now forgiven from sin through the shed blood of Jesus, whoever believes in the Son is going to get the eternal life that he has. This is a heavenly life, the life of the Father, Son and Spirit. What a great mystery this is. Thankfully, the Lord helps us to understand it in some measure through the greatness of his name.

In Genesis 1:1 in the Hebrew Scriptures, we first encounter our Creator God as Elohim. The Hebrew scriptures say this, "In the beginning, Elohim created the heavens and the earth..." In this context, this name carries the meaning of One Spirit in Plural. Our creator God is referred to in this way 32 times in Genesis 1 alone and 2500 times in the whole Old Testament. Our God wants us to know that he is one but that he is plural. We can know him as Father, as Son and as Spirit. This is the life that is offered to us through Jesus Christ.

Where is Life?

If Jesus has that life, and he's going to offer it to us, let's consider where that life is. John 5:26 says this, "For just as the Father has life in himself, even so He gave to the Son to have life in Himself." Make a note: The Father has life in himself. He keeps his glorious, divine, creative life inside of him. Then he gave Jesus the same way to operate. He gave the Son to have life...in himself. When you see Jesus operating, you see a human living out of the glorious, divine, creative life of his Father inside of him.

And now, through the death and resurrection of Jesus Christ, in one of the most significant developments of human history, when we receive Jesus Christ, we receive that life into ourselves. OK, I get it. Life is "IN" for me, too. God invites me to have this same life in myself through Christ Jesus. That's pretty awesome!

This passage later tells us in verses 39 and 40, "You (the Pharisees) search the Scriptures because you think in them you'll have eternal life... but you are unwilling to come to me so that you may have life." The Pharisees thought, "If I just study the scrolls of the Old Testament, I'll understand the mysteries of life." But the Lord said, "Those bear witness of me, but you're unwilling to come to me that you may have life!" The Pharisees came to the Old Testament Scriptures thinking that by diligently studying them and following their rules, they would find life. But they were mistaken; so mistaken that when the one with real life came along, they did not recognize him.

Jesus explained this to the Pharisee Nicodemus in John chapter 3. To his credit, Nicodemus knew there was something unique about Jesus. He secretly came to see Jesus to find out what enabled him to live as he did. Interestingly, he began the conversation by talking about Jesus' behavior: "No one can do these signs that you do unless God is with him" (John 3:2). In other words, who are you and what is your secret for living? Watch where the Lord takes him, "Truly, truly, I say to you, unless one is born from above, he cannot see the kingdom of God." Jesus cuts right to the chase. Notice there is no mention of behavior in his answer. Instead, Jesus talks about being born out of the heavens, thereby receiving a new life. Jesus knows that if he gives the religiously minded Nicodemus an option for some kind of behavior based Christianity, he will take it. If there is a way to live this life by keeping rules or performing, Nicodemus will pursue it.

But Jesus goes to the central issue. If Nicodemus wanted to experience the benefits of living in the kingdom of God, if he wanted to understand the secret of Jesus, he had to receive a new life. The same goes for you and me. There is an important observation to be made here: we ought not to introduce people to living the life Jesus has for us by focusing them on behavior. We should follow Jesus' lead and tell them about the new life that he offers to us.

Life: God's Purpose from the Beginning

The desire of God to share his life with us was present from the beginning of creation. How do we know that? In Genesis 2:9, as part of the creation account we learn that for the sustenance of the man he had made, the Lord caused all kinds of trees to grow in the Garden of Eden that were both pleasing to the eye and good for food.

Then he placed two trees in the middle of that garden, the tree of life and the tree of the knowledge of good and evil. In Genesis 2:16, God told Adam that he could eat from any tree in the garden. In fact, he told him to "freely eat." There was one exception to that invitation, the tree of knowledge of good and evil. Eating from that tree would result in death.

We are likely familiar with how that sad story ended. Deceived by God's enemy, Satan, Eve and then Adam with her, took in the fruit of the wrong tree, thus disobeying the Lord, and causing their downfall. Their choice allowed sin to enter the world and lodge in their fleshly bodies. Passed on from parents to children this ensured we would all be sinners by nature. All of us are well aware of the fact that we are not perfect. Instead of receiving the life that was in the tree of life, mankind fell and lost intimacy with the Creator God. The broken world that resulted is all around us.

But, on the other side, have you ever stopped to consider what kind of life was in the tree of life? This amazing tree contained the eternal, divine life of God himself. Our Lord, through the tree of life, actually made himself available to the man and woman he had created. But, as noted, they did not eat of that tree. Instead they ate of the tree that God had warned them not to eat. As a result, they got the knowledge of good and evil but without the life that would have made them whole. Through their disobedience mankind was infected with sin. Adam and Eve died spiritually and as Genesis 3 tells us, God had to close the way to the tree of life, lest they eat from it and live forever in their fallen state. What a disaster that would have been!

But God's purpose to get his life into the man he created would not be thwarted. God's promise of life would not be made void. He had been waiting too long for that. Consider this statement from the Apostle Paul writing to his co-worker Titus around 66 AD," Paul, a bond servant of God and an apostle of Jesus Christ, for the faith of those chosen of God and the knowledge of the truth which is according to godliness, in hope of eternal Life, which God, who cannot lie, promised before times eternal." Who did he make that promise to? Evidently to himself. And to his creation in waiting. And since his being includes Father, Son and Spirit, the Lord had the means to fulfill the promise. He would not turn his back on mankind, despite their failure.

This purpose, promised by the Creator God before time and pictured in Genesis 2, was brought into focus with the coming of the Lord Jesus in the flesh. He came to share his life with us and to re-open the way to the tree of life. Jesus himself would become the source of God's divine life for all who would believe. This remains his purpose in time and eternity. Take a look at these closing words of the New Testament in Revelation 22:14, "Blessed are those who wash their robes, so they might have the right to the Tree of Life and may enter by the gates into the city." Our God's purpose in Genesis and indeed, before times eternal, becomes full reality in the heavenly Jerusalem.

But What About Now? How Are We to Live?

Too often believers think that while their salvation in Christ cannot be earned, following him means working hard at becoming better Christians. That frame of mind leads to a life of comparing yourself to other Christians. But if you receive life and your neighbor receives life, which one of you has more of Jesus? Whoever has more is bound to be a better Christian, right?

But there aren't any quantities mentioned. There is not one verse in the New Testament that talks about having more of Jesus than someone else. You have life in you if you believe. I have life in me if I believe. Which one of us has more of this life? Neither! Remember, this life is Jesus, himself. Therefore, we both have the same access to Jesus. You've got him, I've got him. It's not based on how intelligent you are or how much knowledge you have. Nor is it based on your emotions, whether you are feeling good or are deeply depressed. He can live just as fully in a carpenter or a computer engineer or a single mom or dad as in a theologian or full-time Christian worker.

What then can be my prayer? "Lord Jesus, be my life. I volunteer to be a person in whom you live abundantly." It helps to keep in mind that when you receive Jesus, you receive him as a seed, "for you have been born again not of seed which is perishable but imperishable, that is, through the living and enduring word of God" (1 Peter 1:23).

A seed is not very big. When you receive new life, the Lord doesn't instantly perfect you, solving all your problems. It may seem that way sometimes in the first blush of your newfound love for the Lord. But as you go on, you discover that living as a Christian is like running an endurance race. Our experience of that life grows as we grow in our understanding and relationship to Jesus Christ. After over fifty years of following him, the Lord is still working patiently and lovingly to infuse my life with his. Thankfully we will have all eternity to fully comprehend all the riches that he is to us.

In John 10:27 and 28, the Lord says this, "My sheep know me. They hear my voice. And I give to them eternal life." Can you see that Jesus Christ is on a mission, not to make you a better person, not to insist that you follow the Ten Commandments, not to make you religious, but to actually get himself into you, for you to know him, to follow him, and to live by him?

What About the Bible?

But what about studying the Bible to know how to live the Christian life? There is no book as unique as the Bible. It stands alone as God's word to mankind. I depend on it for refreshment, revelation and fellowship with the Lord.

But there are times when the Bible can lose its vitality. Has that happened to you? This may be because we have sought head knowledge rather than life in its pages. We may be looking to the Scriptures primarily for guidelines, as truth to be gained, not as the doorway to the one who is our life. Alternately, and sadly, the Bible's words may be a source of guilt for us because they have been used many times to tell us what we ought to be doing and probably aren't, or what we shouldn't have done but might have.

Suppose you have sought to be a good Christian, diligently reading the Bible and working hard to put what you have read into practice. But something has been missing. You are making a noble effort. At times that approach seems to work, but over the course of time you grow weary of the effort. I remember once having to read through the Bible in order to be confirmed as a church member. It seemed like such an arduous ordeal! I did not experience life. What was wrong?

I was missing Jesus' point. Real life is found in him. Thank God we can touch life through reading the Scriptures. That has never been in dispute. But we do that by linking the Scriptures with the living Jesus. So as you come to the Scriptures, invite the living Lord into your presence. As the Lord meets you, you are going to touch real life. Nicodemus found the way to the Savior. So can we.

Life versus Scriptural Correctness

The Pharisees didn't connect the Scriptures with the living Lord who stood before them. And if we fail to connect the Scriptures with the resurrected Christ, we're going to have the same result. This explains why sincere believers can use the Bible in ways that divide the body of Christ rather than build it up. The problem is that I study the Scriptures and find one thing, and someone else studies and finds something else. If the two of us disagree strongly enough, we declare theological war. And we don't quit until everyone in our circles of influence is doctrinally dead. In the process, the unity and life that Christ died and rose again to bring is nowhere to be found.

At last count according to the World Christian Encyclopedia there are at least 9000 ways Christians have figured out how to denominate themselves. When independent churches are included, some sources place the number as high as 33,000. Can such a statistic please the Lord? Is there a road that can lead us to unity despite our differences of opinion?

Yes! We find common ground by seeking life, Christ's life. But, instead of life, other things have been elevated: knowledge, doctrine, miracles, emotional experience, etc. We can have all these but miss having the living Jesus shared between us. Where is the consideration of whether life is produced? If the result of our study doesn't produce life, we would be wise to stop and ask, "Lord, have I found you in this?"

The point is that if I allow my doctrine to separate me from another believer to the extent that we cannot have fellowship in Christ, indeed to the point where we harbor animosity toward one another or look down on one another, then I've settled for something less than life. We are not speaking here about core issues of the Christian faith such as redemption, forgiveness of sin, the resurrection of the Lord Jesus, the indwelling of the Holy Spirit and the inspiration of the Scriptures. No, we are addressing things that have separated believers from one another, such as church organization, varying beliefs on baptism, the gifts of the Spirit, whether believers can drink wine or play cards and on and on. There is a higher way.

God's Higher Way

Jesus showed us life on a higher plane in his encounter with a woman from Samaria. This is recorded in John, chapter 4. Under normal conditions a Jewish man would have nothing to do with a Samaritan woman. Indeed, it was considered illegal to do so. Jews considered Samaritans to be a mixed race, only partly Jewish, with religious roots steeped in idolatry. They had their own center of worship on a mountain called Gerizim. The hatred between them was strong. John himself said that Jews "had no dealings with the Samaritans" (John 4:9). It was in a Samaritan village that Jesus' disciples wanted to rain down fire from heaven because they wouldn't receive Jesus as he was traveling to Jerusalem (Luke 9:52-54).

It was in this context that Jesus approached a local woman at a well in Samaria and asked her for a drink. She was shocked that he would speak to her, much less ask her for a drink. But it was all a setup. Jesus wanted to offer her water. But what amazing water it was.

Here is how he described it, "Whoever drinks of the water that I will give him shall never thirst; but the water that I give him will become in him a well of water, springing up to eternal life" (John 4:14). Drinking this water, Jesus said, gives a person an ongoing supply of the water of life. What kind of life? Eternal life, divine life, his life.

Jesus described his encounter with this woman to his disciples in this way, "Already he who reaps is receiving wages and is gathering fruit for life eternal, so that he who sows and he who reaps may rejoice together" (John 4:36).

From these words we can infer that before Jesus even encountered that particular Samaritan woman, his father God had been sowing seeds into her life. One day Jesus came along to do the reaping. He didn't care that she was one of the hated Samaritans. He loved her.

Jesus wasn't confined by the cultural taboos regarding talking with women. And while he was certainly well acquainted with the brokenness of her past, that didn't stop him from engaging her either. What would be the result of this sowing and reaping? This Samaritan woman would eventually receive the eternal life of God through the coming of the Holy Spirit.

What's great about this whole scene is that this is what the Father, Son and Spirit love to do. They love to share their life with men and women who are desperately in need of it. And when that happens, they rejoice together. If you are a believer, our Elohim rejoiced on the day when you received the water of life. And make no mistake; the Lord continues to rejoice over you today.

Let's consider how much fruit was gathered as a result of this offering of life. The woman went back to her village and told everyone there about Jesus. As a result, many more wanted to hear from him. So Jesus spent two more days with them sharing the message of life. As a result, many more believed in him (John 4: 39, 41). Later on, after the Lord's death and resurrection, the apostles preached the gospel in Samaria and the Holy Spirit gloriously fell on those who heard the message (Acts 8 14-25). Surely those who had believed in Jesus through his encounter with the Samaritan woman would have been among that number. Fellowships were established in these villages that grew and prospered.

Later on, Paul, the former Pharisee and Samaritan hater, visited the fellowships in Samaria, sharing the good news of what God was doing in Gentile lands and encouraging these believers, now numbered among his brothers and sisters in Christ (Acts 15:3). The living water that the Lord offered to the woman at the well was now springing up all over the parched land of Samaria.

Jesus paid a price for reaching out to the Samaritan woman. Later on in an encounter with the Jews from Jerusalem, they even called him a Samaritan, their equivalent of a half-breed, and said he had a demon (John 8:48). Jesus paid no mind. He didn't just bear the contempt that came from speaking with that woman. He bore all of our contempt as he went to the cross, was resurrected and then returned to fulfill his goal: giving us life.

Jesus' death on the cross and his glorious resurrection are at the center of the Lord's work on our behalf. Here is how the Apostle Paul put it when writing to the Corinthians, "For I delivered to you as of first importance what I also received, that Christ died for our sins according to the Scriptures, and that he was buried and that he was raised on the third day." (1 Corinthians 15:3-4) That which the Lord gave to Paul of first importance is that the Lord Jesus shed his blood to cover our sin, went into the grave and was gloriously resurrected so that he could return to live in us.

What a cost Jesus paid at the cross! The terrible word excruciating comes from Jesus' experience there. The word itself comes from the Latin ex crucio which means "out of the cross." What motivated Jesus to endure that suffering? An eternal abiding love. Jesus went through the agony of the cross because of his and his father's love for us. God's life is the source of love; his love for us and by extension, our love for others. That's wonderful to know. Now we don't have to try and "love our neighbors as ourselves," something that never worked very well for me. In our strength we cannot pull that off. But, thank God, Jesus in us can. He has already proved that at the cross. What is the source for offering real love to others? Knowing Jesus as our life!

God Makes It Practical

How does the Lord make it practical? Knowing that we would need some help in understanding this truth, the Lord presented himself in a form everyone can relate to:

Food.

In John 6, the Lord fed five thousand people who had been following him around, listening to him teach. He went away but the people continued to follow him. When they found him the next day, they wanted another free meal. He said, "Don't work for the food which perishes, work for the food which results in eternal life, which the Son of Man shall give to you (John 6:27)." He made a connection between life and food. There was a food that produced real life.

In this same passage, the Lord made it clear that he would be that food when he presented himself as bread. Here is what he said in John 6:35, "I am the bread of Life; he who comes to me will not hunger and he who believes in me will never thirst." His words made it clear that he was the bread of God come down out of heaven to give life to the world. The Lord Jesus was letting them and us know that he is real food, spiritual food, and that by eating him we will have real life.

Have you exhausted yourself looking for the key that gives meaning to life? Never-ending ads offer products that promise all we are looking for. But they don't deliver. Maybe you've fasted, taken on a Bible study program, followed a Biblical weight loss regimen, read a good book on Christian living, or committed to a special season of prayer. In their own right and in the right season, these can all be beneficial. But often, you've found that not much has changed. You might be working too hard through your own effort and not relying on Jesus to be your energy source. By presenting himself as the living bread the Lord Jesus showed us the connection between making him our food and experiencing life.

He continued to make the point when he said, "As the living Father sent me and I live by the Father, so he who eats me shall live by me" (John 6:57-58). What an incredible statement! It sounds so easy. All we have to do is make the Lord our food and we will live by him.

But how do we do that?

One simple starting point is to open your mouth and call on the Lord. Call to him during your day. Let his name be on your lips as you encounter stress. As you sense the Lord's nearness, you can tell him you love him. This opens the way to spending time in his presence, listening for guidance and fellowshipping with him. Thank him for the things that come your way. Invite him to speak to you about how he feels about you.

The Scriptures tell us, "Open your mouth and I will fill it" (Psalm 81:10). Your relationship with the Lord as life starts in the heart, not the brain. Jesus is in you and wants to be your life. Respond to him by inviting him to be your life in the daily decisions that come your way. I remember once facing a responsibility that I felt the Lord was asking me to do. I did not feel qualified nor did I have the desire to carry it out. So, in a time of fellowship with him, I asked him why he wanted me to do that. His answer still warms my heart. "Because you are my friend," he said. That changed everything. I gladly went through with it, looking to my friend Jesus for wisdom in carrying out the details.

A second way to make Jesus your food is to spend time in his written Word. Allow the Christ who is in your heart to bring to life the God-breathed words of the Scriptures. Ask the Lord to reveal himself to you in his word and to touch you with his life. Then begin to read. When you sense his presence, stop and talk to him. Then, let him speak to you. There will come a sense of life, and when you sense that life, you will know it.

A third way to access the life of Jesus within you is to spend time with other believers. Jesus is life to believers in every situation, no matter where we find ourselves. But in the big picture, the Lord designed us to be part of his body. To go beyond understanding the meaning of the word "life" into a richer experience of that life, find some Christian friends who also want to know the Lord as life. For most people, it's more enjoyable to share a great meal with friends than to eat one alone. Experiencing Jesus is no different. Corporate worship and sharing in the Lord's presence is a healing and refreshing way to enjoy our Jesus. As Psalm 22:3 tells us, "The Lord is enthroned on the praises of his people."

The Mind Set on the Spirit is Life

Jesus Christ lives in believers through the Holy Spirit. The Lord introduced his followers to that coming reality at the Feast of Pentecost in Jerusalem recorded in John 7. On the last day of that great feast, attended by hundreds of thousands of Israelites, Jesus stood above the crowds and yelled out, "If anyone is thirsty, let him come to me and drink. He who believes in me, as the Scripture said, from his innermost being will flow rivers of living water." The Lord had already presented himself as the Bread of Life in John 6. Now in John 7 he declared himself the Water of Life as well. But how will that work? The Scriptures describe it this way, "But this he spoke of the Spirit, whom those who believed in him were to receive, for the Spirit was not yet given, because Jesus was not yet glorified."

According to these words, Jesus had to be crucified and go to the grave for the forgiveness of our sin. With that accomplished, the Lord Jesus was raised from the dead, ascended to his Father and was glorified in his presence. From that glorious position he has returned to live in his followers through the Holy Spirit. This is what Paul meant when he wrote in 1 Corinthians 15:45, "The first man, (Adam) was made a living soul, the last Adam (Jesus Christ) became the life giving Spirit." That's pretty amazing. Jesus can now live in us through his mighty Spirit, giving us his life! Paul confirmed this for us in Colossians 1:27 when he wrote the following about believers in Christ, "To whom God willed to make known what are the riches of the glory of this mystery among the nations, which is Christ in you, the hope of glory!"

With this in mind we can be helped by remembering these words in Romans 8:6, "The mind set on the Spirit is life and peace." As you learn how to set your mind on the Spirit within, you are going to have a sense of life, a sense of peace. The Lord uses that inner guidance to lead you.

That said, we can find ourselves involved in actions or relationships that leave us feeling troubled. We may say something or have something said to us that results in the same kind of inner distress. It happens. As a result, we will have an internal heaviness. There won't be a sense of life. There won't be the presence of peace.

What do we do in those times? That is the time to run to the Lord and say, "Lord, you live in me. I confess that something is wrong. There's no life, there's no peace." Turn within and ask for forgiveness or for clarity and wisdom. Respond to what Jesus seems to be asking of you as you rest in him. Invite the Holy Spirit to free you up from whatever is holding you down. Then you can find the life and peace within that Jesus offers. This process may take some time as our will also wants to assert itself and will try and take charge. But eventually, through the Lord's help, we will realize we cannot work things out on our own. Our hope is in our forgiving and living Lord.

In John 20:31, the apostle John reminded us, "The reason I wrote this book is that you might believe and, believing, that you might have life in his (Jesus') Name." Jesus Christ came because he wanted to pour his life into you. An understanding and experience of the life of Jesus in us is central to releasing the divine activity of God in us and discovering the richness and fullness of who he is.

Your calling is not to remember the Ten Commandments. Your calling is not to try to be a good Christian. Your calling is to fellowship with Jesus Christ as much as possible. He is real life in you, and you are changed by feeding on him.

The Lord's Purpose Revealed

John 17 brings this study of life to its high note. The Lord was about to go to the cross. He had gathered his closest friends for final instructions. Surely what was foremost on his heart was going to come out. Here is how the chapter begins, "These things Jesus spoke and lifting up his eyes to heaven, he said, "Father, the hour has come; glorify your Son that the Son may glorify you, even as you gave him authority over all mankind, that to all whom you have given him, he may give eternal life. This is eternal life: that they may know you, the only true God, and Jesus Christ, whom you have sent" (John 17: 1-3).

Jesus made his purpose clear. The Father gave the Son the authority to give life to all those who believe in him. The whole purpose of Jesus' coming to Earth is centered here. If you have received this life, you have an open invitation to get to know the Father and the Son in intimate ways. If you had an invitation to get to know an incredibly creative artist or the best of the world's leaders, doubtless you would want to do that. This offer from our Lord to share his life is even better because he is the Creator God and the King of Kings.

What is eternal life? It is really not that complicated. Eternal life is found in knowing God the Father, God the Son and God the Holy Spirit living inside of us. He is our Elohim, the One Spirit in plural. On a practical level, remember that life is not separate from Jesus. If you have an experience of life, you have had an experience with the Lord. If you have sensed life in a song or a story shared by a fellow believer or in the Scriptures or in a moment of real need when the Lord has given you peace, you have had an experience with Jesus Christ. Whenever you are enjoying the fruits of the Spirit like love, joy, patience, kindness and long suffering, you are sharing in the life of Jesus inside you. As the Lord himself said, "I am the way, the truth and the life." Thank God, we don't have to wait until eternity to know eternal life. That life is ours today in Jesus Christ.

If you are a believer in Jesus, in your spirit right now there is a life that's divine. That life is Jesus Christ, himself. When you turn to him, he is there for you. He can fill and direct your thoughts, he can inspire and touch your emotions. He is a person who is life.

If you will go through the Gospel book of John, you will see many references to your Lord as life. Once you have seen your Lord as the new life that is in you, that opens new doors of fellowship with him. Will it come easily? No, you can expect a fight. God's enemy will seek to minimize the greatness of your Lord and his power to work in you. But press on! He has come that you may have life. If you are not sure if you have ever received this life, stop now and invite the Lord Jesus to come and live in you. Confess your need for him and ask him to fill your heart with his Spirit. He will hear and answer your prayer. So begins the greatest relationship that can be known in time and eternity...

The Spirit

"Unless you are born of water and the Spirit …" John 3:5

The Creator God, our Elohim, has the wonderful plan of establishing his heavenly kingdom here on Earth. To that end, He designed a practical way to build that kingdom that allows us to partake and participate in it. In fact, for many years those who first followed Jesus into kingdom life were known as "The Way." Central to our understanding and experience of the way into that kingdom is the person of the Spirit.

Many believers are unclear about the person and role of the Spirit. Doctrinal differences over the meaning of the Baptism of the Holy Spirit and the modern-day practice of the gifts of the Spirit, for example, have divided and perplexed many believers. As a result, many followers of Jesus have been scared away from an active relationship with the Spirit perhaps even having been taught that the gifts of the Spirit ceased after the first century or when the Bible was put together. Not surprisingly, they are often left with a Christian experience that lacks vitality. Why is that? Simply put, the Spirit brings the vital presence of God into our lives.

In this regard, a Biblical understanding of the Spirit is a great help in having a revitalized experience with Jesus, both for us personally and in our circles of fellowship. Focusing on that is my goal here.

The Importance of the Spirit

The Lord Jesus said to Nicodemus in John 3: 5: "Truly, truly, I say to you, unless one is born of water and of the Spirit, he cannot enter into the kingdom of God. That which is born of the flesh is flesh; and that which is born of the Spirit is Spirit." If we are going to experience the benefits of living in the kingdom of God, we must be born of the Spirit. That means that access to the kingdom is only possible through the Spirit. John the Baptizer said, "I am baptizing in repentance, but the one that comes afterwards, he will baptize in the Holy Spirit." Repentance opens the way for us to begin a new relationship with our God and to develop a new mindset regarding what He is like. According to what Jesus said to Nicodemus, leaving human efforts to reach God behind, and developing a new way of relating to Him is made possible through the Spirit.

Jesus' mission as introduced by John in his Gospel, was directly related to his followers being baptized or, perhaps more aptly translated, immersed, in this Spirit. John didn't say that Jesus was going to immerse some in the Spirit and not others. Nor do the Scriptures say that being immersed in the Spirit is a second blessing of some kind, reserved for those who are really serious about following Jesus. As Paul wrote to the Corinthians, "For by one Spirit we are all baptized into one body, whether we be Jews or Gentiles, whether we be bond or free; and we have all been made to drink of one Spirit" (I Corinthians 12:13).

In my years as the overseas director for a large Christian missions organization, I received many letters from ministry leaders overseas. Some of them, when describing an outreach, would write such things as "500 people received the Lord and 75 of them were baptized in the Holy Spirit." It was obvious they were really happy about the 75. But what about the rest? Were they some kind of second-class Christian citizens? How would they live the Christian life without the Spirit? That never made much sense to me. If you've received the Lord, how have you received him if not through the Spirit?

From John's words we can see that baptizing or immersing all of his followers in the Holy Spirit was central to Jesus' purpose in coming to this planet. So who is this Spirit, and how does he work? A good place to start might be to ask what your comfort level is with respect to the

Holy Spirit. If you had to rate your level of comfort regarding the Divine Trinity of Father, Son and Spirit, which one would you say that you are more drawn to? Is there one that you feel more comfortable with, one that you would consider as having a higher level of importance in your life as a Christian?

When this question is asked in Christian settings, inevitably, those present answer that they feel most comfortable with the Son, the Lord Jesus. Most people feel drawn to the Son. This is totally understandable. The Lord Jesus is the one who put on human flesh and whose life we see recorded in the gospels. The Lord Jesus is the One who died for our sins. The Lord Jesus is the One who has given us new life.

What often happens, however, is that people tend to identify only with the Jesus of the Gospels. He's the Jesus that walked on earth, the Jesus that changed water into wine, and the Jesus on the cross. They tend to associate Jesus primarily with the physical human being that walked the dusty roads of Galilee in the first century.

But is there a more intimate way to relate to him now that believers have underutilized because they have not seen the totality of God's nature? They love Jesus, they understand Jesus, but they don't understand the Spirit very well, so they just don't go there.

God, our Elohim, is Comfortable as Spirit

It helps to understand that God the Father has always been Spirit. He is absolutely comfortable being Spirit, and wants us to know him as such. Jesus emphasized this in John 4:24 when he said, "God is Spirit and those who worship him must worship him in Spirit and in truth." Before God the Son became incarnate, he was also Spirit. These two were wonderfully, divinely one.

We have covered this earlier, but consider again the Name of Elohim, the one Spirit in plural, used in the book of Genesis. Our Creator God is Father. He is Son and He is Spirit. Though difficult for our minds to comprehend, our God wants us to know the mystery that the three are one. Consider the apostle John's opening words in his gospel, "In the beginning was the Word and the Word was toward God (Elohim) and the Word was God (Elohim). He was in the beginning with Elohim. All things came into being through him and apart from him nothing came into being that has come into being…and the Word became flesh and dwelt among us." It was through this divine Word that God created the universe and, wondrously enough, one day this Word became flesh as the incarnate Son of God, Jesus Christ.

Prior to his incarnation, this divine Word was Spirit. And out of his spiritual richness, the vast variety of the universe came into being. When we see the incredible beauty of the creation, we should be mindful that its inspiration came out of invisible realms. As the writer of Hebrews put it, "By faith we understand that the worlds were prepared by the Word of God so that what is seen was not made out of things which are visible" (Heb. 11:3).

The realm of the Spirit and the realm of the physical have always been intertwined in the plan of God. In Genesis 1, the Spirit of God was present, moving over the face of the waters. And out of this glorious Spirit came the created universe. Its complexity only hints at the variety and richness in our God. Do you love sunsets? Those sunsets portray something of the spiritual richness of God. Do you love horses or dogs or waterfalls or moonlit nights? All the qualities that make them lovable or beautiful or enchanting were born out of his vibrant being. The wonder of it all is that God desires to offer the riches of his Spirit-filled realm to us.

But therein lies a problem. God is Spirit. But what is man? According to Genesis 2:7, "The Lord God formed man of dust from the ground and breathed into his nostrils the breath of life and man became a living soul."

God in his essence is Divine Spirit. Man in his created essence is soul. The apostle Paul refers to this when he says in I Corinthians 15:45, "The first man Adam was made a living soul." Soul can be defined as the human personality made up of those characteristics of mind, emotion, and will that motivate human beings. Adam's human soul was encased in a body made of earth that we call flesh. In fact, the word "Adam" meant red clay.

How will a Creator God who is Spirit transmit the riches of his realm to a man who is soul? Or, to put it another way, who will bridge the gap between Spirit and soul? In the Genesis creation the answer lay in God's provision of the tree of life. God placed his own life into the

Garden in the Tree of Life. He invited man to eat of every tree of the garden except the Tree of the Knowledge of Good and Evil. If man had partaken of the Tree of Life and taken into himself the life contained therein, he would have had access to the riches of God's life. But man failed to do that and ate instead of the forbidden tree. Man fell from his high position as God's selected image-bearer and God closed the way to the Tree of Life. In the process man lost his connection to God and became preoccupied with the physical and earthly.

Thus began the history of mankind. But our Creator God, our Elohim, never wavered in his purpose of making the riches of his spirit realm available to his creation. The fullness of that plan was realized in time with the coming of Jesus Christ. Jesus brought the reality of God's realm to earth. His birth, life, death and resurrection were the glorious product of a human life saturated by the divine life of the Spirit of God. He was God come in flesh, the image of the invisible God. But how would God's purpose play out following the ascension of Jesus?

Jesus Shows the Way

Understanding the difficulty with which we humans grasp spiritual realities, just before Jesus went to the cross he sought to help his disciples prepare for what was ahead. He said, "I will ask the Father and he will give you another Helper that he may be with you forever, the Spirit of Truth, whom the world cannot receive, because it does not see him or know him; you know him because he abides with you and will be in you. I will not leave you as orphans, I will come to you" (John 14:16-18).

Jesus made it plain to his disciples that though he would be physically leaving them, help was on the way. He had not simply given them a model by which to live, so that now that they had seen Jesus in action, they should be able to do the same things. No. The Spirit of Truth was coming, who would never leave them. But who was this Spirit of Truth that Jesus would give this important task to? Look at his words: "You know him because he abides with you and will be in you...I will come to you." Yes, the Spirit of Truth is Jesus, himself. This is only possible because of the plural nature of our Creator God, Elohim.

Listen to Jesus' words to his Father in John 17:22-24: "The glory which you have given Me, I have given to them, that they may be one, just as We are one, I in them and You in Me, that they may be perfected in unity so that the world may know that you sent me and loved them even as you have loved me."

These incredibly mysterious and deep words make it clear who is going to be in us. Jesus says, "I in them." It was always Jesus' intention to make the realm of the spiritual accessible to those who would believe in him so that they could continue to be with him. Jesus is not in us simply to occupy space. He is not in us simply to forgive us of our sins. No. he wants to take us where he is, into his Father's heavenly presence. Now.

Listen to this description of Jesus in John 7:37: "Now on the last day, the great day of the feast, Jesus stood and cried out saying, if anyone is thirsty, let him come to me and drink. He who believes in me, as the Scripture says, from his innermost being will flow rivers of living water. But this he spoke of the Spirit, whom those who believed in him were to receive; the Spirit was not yet given, because Jesus was not yet glorified."

Let's put this event in context to see how truly meaningful Jesus' words were. The feast being celebrated here was the Feast of Booths or Tabernacles. It was the most celebratory of all the feasts. By this time, a special water ceremony had become part of the tradition of the festival. This was called the "Simchat Beit Hashoavah" – the water-drawing festival. The priests would go down to the pool of Siloam in the City of David and fill a golden vessel with water. Then they would go up to the temple, through the Water Gate, accompanied by the sound of the shofar, and they would pour the water so that it flowed over the altar, along with wine from another bowl. This would begin the prayers for much needed seasonal rain. All week long the Jewish people would be looking forward to the water ceremony. In fact, in describing that part of the feast, the Talmud, part of the Jewish law, described it like this:

"He who has not seen the rejoicing at the place of the water-drawing has never seen rejoicing in his life." It's significant that the ceremony also referred to this passage in Isaiah 12: "***Behold, God is my salvation; I will trust, and will not be afraid; for the Lord God is my strength and my song, and he has become my salvation. With joy you will draw water from the wells of salvation." (Isaiah 12:2-3)***

One of the names for this day was "Hoshana Raba", which meant Great Salvation. Now consider that this is the exact word for Jesus' name – Salvation. The Hebrew scripture literally says, "with joy you will draw water from the wells of Yeshua!" That is the context in which Jesus stood up at the end of the feast days and shouted out to the assembled masses, "If you are thirsty, come to me and drink!" What a bold thing to do. What an incredible fulfillment of the Old Testament picture.

The weeklong Feast of Booths was coming to an end. The Jews had been eating and drinking for days. Jesus knew that satisfaction could not be found simply in outward, earthly pleasures. He knew there was deep thirst in the human soul for something that went beyond the physical, the earthly. In the same way, he knows that in your soul there is a longing for things spiritual, for things divine. That longing has been present in the human soul since the day of its creation.

Jesus stood in the midst of the vast throng and called all who were thirsty to come to him to drink. By so doing, he invited all who were thirsty for real life to come to him. He is the source of our water of life. He is our drink, our sustenance. He is the fulfillment of the water drawing ceremony! Jesus was not talking about himself in physical form. He was not inviting people to come to the earthly Jesus, the Jesus who walked in Galilee. No, he was inviting those who thirst for real water to come to the Spirit. He was talking about water that would be drunk in Spirit. He, himself, would be that water! But this Spirit was not yet available to them, for Jesus was not yet glorified.

Who Will Lead God's People?

Consider the Lord's words in John 10: "He who enters by the door is a shepherd of the sheep. To him the doorkeeper opens and the sheep hear his voice and he calls his own sheep by name and leads them out. When he puts forth all his own he goes ahead of them and the sheep follow him because they know his voice... v.16 I have other sheep who are not of this flock, I must bring them also and they shall hear my voice and they shall become one flock with one shepherd."

Jesus is the good shepherd. Those who follow him will hear his voice. That is how he will lead them. He knows all their names. This is very personal and very precious. Jesus laid down his life to achieve the awesome ability to lead each of his followers in this most direct of ways. This didn't pertain to only the Jewish believers who followed him around Galilee. The Lord had other sheep that were not Jewish that he wanted to hear his voice; that he longed to lead into heavenly, spiritual realms. You are one of those sheep. He laid down his life and took it back again so that we could know him as our shepherd.

But there is a mystery here. How will the earthly Jesus become the spiritual water of life? How will the earthly Jesus speak to those born in later ages, leading them into his gracious presence? Here's the answer.

Jesus, the Life Giving, Love Producing Spirit

Going back to the beginning of creation, remember that God is not only love, He is a lover. Out of his love, God decided to have a family. He would do that by creating a bride for his Son. To that end, our Creator God, Elohim, created man and woman and placed them in the Garden where He also made his life available to them. Out of that union would come the family God desired. But, as we know, man fell and sin entered the human race. Now God had two issues to deal with. First, man was created a living soul and needed a way to access spiritual realms. Second, when man fell he became sinful. In such a state he could never gain entrance into the presence of a holy God. When a sinless Jesus was crucified for us, he bore our sins. Those accepting his shed blood have a remedy for sin. The issue of sin dealt with, here's how the Father gives his cleansed children access to spirit living. Paul described it in I Corinthians 15:45: "The first man Adam became a living soul; the last Adam, a life giving Spirit." God the Father desired to fill the universe with the riches that are contained in his wondrous being. Those riches were stored in his Son, Jesus Christ, come in the flesh, born as the Son of Man. In Christ, the living, loving God could enter the realm of the physical and create a means of access to the divine.

In Jesus' resurrection and ascension, his earthly body was transformed to the point where the physical no longer constrained him. Jesus previewed this in his prayer to the Father in John 17 when he said, "Father, glorify me now with the glory that I had with you before the world ever was." When Jesus came to his planet, he laid down his eternal, spiritual glory. As Philippians describes it, "although he existed in the form of God, he did not regard equality with God something to be held onto, but he emptied himself, taking the form of a bond slave."

So what happened to Jesus? We see the story laid out for us in the gospels. Watch Jesus' interactions with his followers following his resurrection. Here's the story. Mary came to the tomb to weep over the Lord she had lost. The One she had come to love with all her heart had been taken from her forever. Or so she thought. She saw the stone rolled away and feared that the body had been taken. She was intensely distraught. She couldn't hold back her tears. She saw someone whom she mistook for the gardener. When she asked him where they had taken her Lord, the resurrected Christ turned and called her name: "Mary."

Mary instantly recognized the tenderness and familiarity in her Lord's voice. She ran to him and clung to him, holding on with all her might, just as you would do if you had lost the person you loved most in the world and suddenly, miraculously, that person had returned to you. But listen to Jesus' surprising words: "Stop clinging to me, for I have not yet ascended to my Father, but go to my brothers and sisters and say to them, I ascend to my Father and your Father and my God and your God." (John 20:17) Through Jesus' death and resurrection, the family of God had expanded. What amazing news!

Mary did as she was told. She ran to let the other disciples know she had seen Jesus. The Lord was alive! Meanwhile the Lord Jesus did just what he said he was going to do. The resurrected Jesus ascended to his Father. There in the Father's presence, in front of the angelic host, Jesus Christ, the Son of Man, was wondrously glorified in the presence of his Father. He who had walked in human flesh was fully transformed with the spiritual glory that he had known with the Father before the earth was formed. His human body was made spiritually divine and, before powers and principalities, the Son of Man was declared to be the Son of God. Human words fail to fully describe what happened there.

Here's how Peter described this event to those present in Jerusalem, "'This Jesus God raised up again, to which we are all witnesses. Therefore, having been exalted to the right hand of God and having received from the Father, the promise of the Holy Spirit, He has poured forth this which you both see and hear. For it was not David who ascended into heaven, but He himself says, The Lord said to my Lord, sit at my right hand, until I make your enemies a footstool for your feet. Therefore, let all the house of Israel know for certain that God had made him (Jesus) both Lord and Messiah, this Jesus whom you have crucified." Jesus, the Son of Man, now enthroned as the Lord of all in the heavens, has returned to Earth through the Holy Spirit to be our Messiah, the head of the church. What a great mystery this is!

Here's how Paul described it to the Romans, "Paul a bond-servant of Christ Jesus, called as an apostle, set apart for the gospel of God, which he promised beforehand through his prophets in the holy Scriptures, concerning his Son who was born of the seed of David according to the flesh who was declared the Son of God with power by the resurrection from the dead according to the Spirit of holiness, Jesus Christ our Lord" (Rom. 1:1-4).

Praise God, a divine human, our king Jesus, is now on the throne of heaven. This is tremendously significant for us. We, who are human, now have the possibility—no, more than that, the expectation—that through our faith in Jesus, we, too, will be glorified in him. What a great work God wrought in Jesus Christ!

Paul put it this way to the Ephesians: "...in accordance with the working of the strength of his [God's] might which he brought about in Christ when he raised him from the dead and seated him at his right hand in the heavenlies, far above all rule and authority and power and dominion and every name that is named not only in this age but also in the one to come, and he put all things in subjection under his feet and gave him as head over all things to the church" (Ephesians 1:19-22).

The crucified, resurrected, ascended and now glorified Jesus returned to the upper room. Meanwhile, his disciples were debating whether or not what they had heard from Mary could possibly be true. Jesus walked through a locked door and into their midst. Then what happened? The disciples freaked out, just as you and I would have done.

But Jesus immediately spoke to their fears. He told them to calm down. Be at peace, he said, and showed them his hands and side.

We might wonder if Jesus couldn't have walked through that door before his death and resurrection. After all, he was God. But the fact of the matter is that there is no record that he did. The Scriptures make it plain that he put on human flesh and humbled himself to become a man. He was tempted in all things, yet without sin. He ate and drank with his friends. He got tired and hungry. He walked over dusty roads. Of course, we would never limit the Lord Jesus, but when he showed up suddenly in the midst of those who knew him best, they were certainly shocked. Something truly divine had happened to their beloved Lord.

Once they realized it was Jesus, they were overjoyed. Pandemonium broke out. Can you imagine the scene? Surely they were grabbing the Lord and taking turns giving him big hugs, just as Mary had in the garden. I'm sure there was a lot of apologizing and asking for forgiveness going on. Undoubtedly, some were saying, "I knew you would be back, I knew it couldn't end like that." Remember, these were emotional disciples who had just gone from the depths of experiencing incredible loss and fear to having their Lord and God returned to them. They loved this man. John says that they rejoiced. We can only imagine.

But what did Jesus do next? Did he tell them to stop clinging to him because he had not yet ascended to his Father? That's what he had earlier said to Mary.

No! On the contrary, he said, "Peace is with you. As the Father has sent me, I also send you." Then he breathed into them and said, "Receive you the Holy Spirit. If you forgive the sins of any, they will be forgiven them; if you retain the sins of any, they have been retained." Both issues resolved. Man can receive the divine Spirit and sins can be forgiven.

Remember what was said at the feast about receiving the living water: "This he spoke of the Spirit, but the Spirit was not yet given because Jesus was not yet glorified." Now that Jesus had been resurrected and glorified in his Father's presence, he was able to dispense his life as Spirit into his disciples. The Spirit could be given because Jesus had been glorified. Now those who are thirsting for real life, wherever they are, wherever they live, can receive the Lord Jesus himself, in Spirit, into them. This is tremendous news. Just as God had been in Christ reconciling the world to himself, now Christ would be in Spirit continuing that ongoing work. This is the wonder of our Creator God, our Elohim, the One Spirit in plural.

Historically, God—the Father, Son and Spirit—had been involved with man in an external way. Throughout the Old Testament record we see God guiding his people, through the burning bush, through the Shekinah glory, through the Urim and the Thummin in the Holy of Holies and through the rock, fire and cloud in the wilderness, to cite a few examples.

Now God, the Divine Trinity, would become one with those who would believe, actually dwelling in them. Jesus shined light on this profound truth in John 17: 20-23, when he prayed, "I do not ask on behalf of these alone, but for those also who believe in me through their word, that they may all be one; as you, Father, are in me, and I in You, that they also may be in us so that the world may believe that You sent me. The glory which You have given me I have given to them; that they may be one, just as we are one; I in them, and You in me, that they may be perfected in unity, that the world may know that You have sent me, and have loved them even as You have loved me." What amazing words! They will take eternity to comprehend.

Paul said it this way in Corinthians 12:13: "For by one Spirit we were all baptized into one body, whether Jews or Greeks, whether slaves or free and we were all made to drink of one Spirit." This was what Jesus was looking forward to as he declared to those Israelites, "Come to me and drink." Throughout the centuries the thirsty have been finding living water at the feet of this glorious Christ. In fact, we were created with this in mind. You and I were designed by God to be able to drink from spiritual realms and glory there in our Lord Jesus. Paul put it this way in Philippians 3:3: "For we are the true circumcision who worship in the Spirit and glory in Christ Jesus and put no confidence in the flesh." And how does all that help our Creator God in his desire to have a family and so spread his love throughout the universe? The Spirit is the vehicle by which that is done. Look at Paul's words from Romans 5:5, "And hope does not disappoint because the love of God has been poured out in our hearts by his Spirit who indwells us." The family of God rooted in the love of God is about to grow!

God's Authority Is in Christ

The Lord spent forty more days with his followers, explaining how life in his kingdom works. Doubtless he told them what it would be like to follow him in Spirit as compared to following him in the flesh. He told them the day would come soon when they would be empowered as the body of Christ with authority by the outward coming of his Spirit on them on the day of Pentecost. Jesus made no secret of where that authority would come from. "All authority has been given to me in heaven and on earth, go therefore and make disciples of all the nations, baptizing them into the Name of the Father and the Son and the Holy Spirit... and, lo, I am with you always, even unto the end of the age" (Matthew 28:18).

What incredibly challenging and yet comforting words: "I am with you always." The glorified Christ, to whom all authority had been given, would be living in his followers through the Spirit, empowering them from within and without to live for him in this world. Christ, the living water that is in our innermost beings, becomes a river of water that springs up out of us and gives real water to a thirsty world.

Paul stated this when he wrote in II Corinthians 3:17, "Now the Lord is the Spirit, and where the Spirit of the Lord is, there is liberty. But we all with unveiled face, beholding as a mirror the glory of the Lord, are being transformed into the same image, from glory to glory, just as from the Lord, the Spirit."

The Scriptures show the intimate connection between the Lord Jesus and the Spirit that resides in us. They are one. To have an experience with the Spirit is to have an experience with Christ. To have an experience with Christ is to have an experience in the Spirit. Paul wrote in I Corinthians 6:17, "The one who joins himself to the Lord is one Spirit with him." We are joined to our Lord in our spirits. He is in us as Spirit. That is why it is so important that we recover the deep meaning of how to live in Spirit.

The Richness of the Spirit

Paul described the all-inclusiveness of this incredible Spirit when he wrote to the Romans, "However, you are not in the flesh, but in the Spirit if indeed the Spirit of God dwells in you. But if anyone does not have the Spirit of Christ, he does not belong to him. If Christ is in you though the body is dead because of sin, yet the Spirit is life because of righteousness. But if the Spirit of him who raised Jesus from the dead dwells in you, he who raised Christ Jesus from the dead will give life to your mortal bodies through his Spirit who indwells you" (Rom 8:9-11). According to this passage the Spirit of God, the Spirit of Christ, Christ, and the Spirit of him who raised Jesus from the dead are all in us. Wow! So how many Spirits are in us?

Only one.

The amazingly wonderful, glorious Lord Jesus through the Spirit brought into us the divine life of his Father God. What a Lord! What a Spirit! Paul longed for God's people to understand this when he wrote to the Ephesians that "through him [Jesus] we have our access in one Spirit to the Father." Jesus is the good shepherd who leads us into his Father's presence, where we can enjoy the riches to be found there: love, joy, peace, patience, long-suffering, kindness, goodness, and self-control.

As Paul wrote in Romans 8:14, "For all who are being led by the Spirit of God, these are sons of God; for you have not received a spirit of slavery leading to fear again, but you have received the Spirit of sonship whereby we cry, Abba, Father (Daddy, Father). The Spirit himself bears witness with our spirit that we are children of God." Does this not sound like our Lord Jesus? He said to his disciples, "Fear not." He said to Mary, "Go and tell my brothers and sisters that I go to my Father and your Father and my God and your God."

This wondrous One who calls "Daddy, Father," from deep within us, bearing witness that we are the children of God, is none other than the Lord Jesus himself, living in us through the Spirit. Paul reminded the Galatians of this when he said, "Because you are sons, God has sent forth the Spirit of his Son into our hearts, crying Abba, Father." Remember Jesus' comforting words to his followers that he would not leave them as orphans, but that he would come to them. Jesus is the One who reunites us with our heavenly Father. If you have the comforting reassurance deep within that you are a child of God, that assurance comes from the Lord Jesus.

The beauty of all this is the uniqueness that we each hold in the Lord's eyes. Each of us is a new creation in Christ, all together making up the body of Christ in all its richness and variety. As Paul wrote in I Corinthians 12:18, "But now, God has placed the members each one of them in the body just as he desired." God loves you deeply and has given you a unique relationship with him. As you join with the Spirit within and call out to him, he makes you complete and the body is built up.

When we see these truths, we don't need to shy away from acknowledging that it is Christ who is the Spirit in us. On the contrary, we welcome him, our Christ and our Lord. As Spirit, Jesus is intimate with us. As Spirit, Jesus is exalted in our midst. As he said in John 15:26, "When the Helper comes, whom I will send to you from the Father, the Spirit of truth, who proceeds from the Father, he will bear witness of me."

When we read the references to the Spirit in the New Testament, it's clear that the first-century believers had a great deal of familiarity with the Lord as Spirit. They felt comfortable talking about the Spirit. They knew they had a spirit and that Christ resided there. They practiced hearing from the Lord in Spirit. They knew that real prayer emanated from the Spirit within them.

Consider this example in Acts 16:6 when Paul traveled to Macedonia: "They passed through the Phrygian and Galatian region having been forbidden by the Holy Spirit to speak the word in Asia and when they had come to Mysia, they were trying to go into Bithynia and the Spirit of Jesus did not permit them." Paul and Silas were called by the Lord to go out and plant churches. They were in great need of his guiding hand. They were not allowed by the Holy Spirit to enter Asia. Then they were kept from entering Bithynia by the Spirit of Jesus. Were there two Spirits they were following? Of course not. The Holy Spirit and the Spirit of Jesus are one. Jesus was alive and well in them, leading his sheep as he promised to do by telling them where to go and where not to go. Thank God, he provides the same kind of leadership today as the Spirit within us.

Making It Practical

Following the Spirit can be dramatic. It can also take much perseverance. But following the Spirit is not an emotional roller coaster ride. It does not involve fear. It is not legalistic. To follow the Spirit is to follow Christ. That's how he leads us.

There are good lessons for us as the family of God to learn here. When we read a verse that exhorts us to "keep the unity of the Spirit in the bond of peace," that sounds like a worthy goal. But if our goal is unity in the Spirit, we evidently don't know how to access that Spirit very well, because believers separate themselves from one another every day. In the United States we have thousands of different church denominations many of whom won't even talk with another. Contrast that with the unity of the Spirit. This is the unity that exists in the Divine Trinity. This is a unity that time, death and eternity will never break. Only a relationship with our Lord in Spirit brings that into our experience with one another.

Much of the New Testament was written to encourage us to a deep understanding of how to access spiritual realms and the experience available there. It was written to help us understand how Christ as the Spirit operates in us. As we turn to him in our spirit and welcome his leadership into our lives, his kingdom is built.

Setting Our Minds on the Spirit

Remembering that the Lord Jesus was Spirit before he was flesh will help us relate to him as Spirit. But the reality is, there is an ongoing choice involved here. Because our first consciousness was of the material world, we must learn a new way of living. As Paul said to the Colossians, we now learn "to set our minds on things above, not on the things of this earth." He exhorted the Romans "that to set the mind on the flesh is death; but to set your mind on the Spirit is life and peace." He encouraged the Corinthians that "we look not at the things which are seen, but at the things which are not seen: for the things which are seen are temporal; but the things which are not seen are eternal" (2 Corinthians 4:18).

Consider also the fascinating words spoken by the Apostle Peter. The Lord brought him to Caesarea to share the good news that Christ was resurrected. This was a major step forward for Peter to bring the gospel to the Gentile nations. Listen to how he spoke about Jesus: "We are witnesses of all the things he did both in the land of the Jews and in Jerusalem. They also put him to death by hanging him on a cross. God raised him up on the third day and granted that he be made visible not to all the people but to witnesses who were chosen beforehand by God, to us who ate and drank with him after he arose from the dead." (Acts 10: 39-41)

God did the first century believers a favor. He granted that Jesus Christ become visible so his disciples could see him for a little while longer. The resurrected, glorified Christ has the ability to be seen or not seen. He has the capacity to be physical or non-physical. He has the ability to move freely between the seen and unseen realms. That is how he can sit on the throne in the Heavens and still be active on earth as head of the church. For the sake of his disciples as they moved from following him in flesh to following him in Spirit, the Lord allowed himself to be seen by them.

Thankfully, Peter was able to make the transition. He got the big picture. Here's what he wrote to the Jews dispersed throughout the Roman Empire: "For Christ also died for sins once for all, the just for the unjust, in order that he might bring us to God, having been put to death in the flesh but made alive in the Spirit" (I Peter 3:18). Peter verified that Jesus Christ is now known by us through the Spirit. He is the Way to the Father.

Here's how Paul described to the Corinthians the transition from following the physical Christ to following the spiritual Christ: "Therefore from now on we recognize no man according to the flesh, even though we have known Christ according to the flesh, yet now we know him thus no longer" (II Corinthians 5:16-17).

In the context of the passage, Paul was talking about how the Corinthians were judging one another according to outward accomplishments. But that is no longer how they were to live. He emphasized the point that they knew Jesus according to the flesh, but now they knew him thus no longer. If they didn't know Jesus according to the flesh, how did they know him? If they weren't thinking about the earthly Jesus who did all the miracles and trying to follow his example, how did they know him?

They knew him in Spirit. They knew him as he wanted to be known—as the living, vibrant Spirit. Jesus did not want to be remembered simply as the Jesus who walked around on the earth in the first century. No, he didn't want to be only remembered as the first century Jesus; he wants to be experienced as the twenty-first century Jesus! That happens in the Spirit.

One day we will see Jesus face to face. Our earthly, physical limitations will be lifted. The Lord will descend out of the heavens with a shout, and we will be like him, for we will see him completely as he is. We will be fully transformed. What a glorious day that will be.

Paul described this in I Corinthians 15:42: "So also is the resurrection of the dead. It is sown perishable; it is raised imperishable; it is sown in dishonor; it is raised in glory: it is sown in weakness; it is raised in power; It is sown an earthly body; it is raised a spiritual body. There is an earthly body, and there is a spiritual body, and so it is written, the first man Adam became a living soul; the last Adam a life giving Spirit; however, the spiritual is not first but the earthly; then the spiritual. The first man is of the earth, earthy: the second man is from heaven; As is the earthy, so also are they that are earthy: and as is the heavenly, so also are those who are heavenly, just as we have borne the image of the earthy, we will also bear the image of the heavenly."

We have a part in seeing that glorious day arrive. God builds his kingdom as we fellowship with him and invite him to work in our lives. As Paul put it to the Ephesians, "And he came and preached peace to you who were far away and peace to those who were near for through him we both have our access in one Spirit to the Father. So then you are no longer strangers and aliens but you are fellow citizens with the saints and are of God's household, having been built on the foundation of the apostles and prophets, Christ Jesus himself being the cornerstone in whom the whole building being fitted together is growing into a holy temple in the Lord, in whom you also are being built together into a dwelling of God in the Spirit." (Ephesians 2:17-22)

My friends claim your birthright. If you are a believer, turn to Jesus in your spirit and fellowship with him there. Allow him to bring you into your heavenly Father's loving presence. In the process, the Lord will build you with other members of his body into his divine family. What an adventure!

Is it easy to follow a Jesus we can't see with our physical eyes? No one who has been at it long would say it is. But the reward is certainly worth the cost. We will need the eyes of our heart to grasp these realities. But, thank God, he is pleased to reveal them to us. As Paul wrote to the Corinthians, "Things which eye has not seen, and ear has not heard, and which have not entered the heart of man, all that God has prepared for those who love him. For to us God revealed them through the Spirit: for the Spirit searches all things even the depths of God." (I. Cor. 2:9-10) His plan is not complicated. It may be mysterious, it may be profound, it may not be easy to apprehend. But it's not complicated.

A good place to start is simply to focus on the words of Paul to the Corinthians. "Now the Lord is the Spirit...." Now, today, your Lord, who sits on the throne in the heavens, is in you as Spirit. Remember he is the ladder that joins heaven and earth. Where he is there is freedom. You are free to meet Christ. You are free to fellowship with him. You are free to go into heavenly realms and fellowship with your majestic Father in the Spirit. This was made possible because the Jesus who lived in the glory of God before time began, and who walked on the earth as the last Adam, went to the grave and was resurrected as the life-giving Spirit. He is our source of forgiveness, of life, of hope, of unity.

One wonderful way to enter into his presence as Spirit is to call out to the Lord. As Paul reminded the Corinthians in I Corinthians 12:3, "No one can say Jesus is Lord, except by the Holy Spirit." As you simply call on the name of the Lord Jesus, you will begin to enjoy the sweetness of his presence.

When you pray, be sensitive to his stirring and speaking within you. When you hear his voice, respond with faith. If you are not sure about something you think the Lord is speaking to you about, talk it over with trusted Christian friends. There is safety in the fellowship of the body of Christ. When you need the Lord's guidance in decision making, move away from any sense of darkness and follow the sense of life and peace, for "the mind set on the Spirit is life and peace."

We are reminded in Psalms 100 to "come before his presence with singing and into his courts with praise." Singing and praising the Lord are also wonderful ways to move from the wanderings of your mind or the stress of your surroundings into his presence. Paul wrote in Colossians 3:16, "Let the word of Christ richly dwell within you with all wisdom teaching and admonishing one another with psalms and hymns and spiritual songs, singing with thankfulness in your hearts to God."

Jesus Christ is alive in his followers through the Holy Spirit. He leads us into fellowship with his Father and into unity with one another. In the process we are made into a dwelling of God in the Spirit through which the nations can see the glory of God and come to their Savior. This move of God began in Jerusalem with the activity of the resurrected and glorified Jesus among his people. It continues today wherever God's people are led by this glorious Spirit.

We have been called to be part of this great adventure. Take some time to stop and ask the Lord to show you your place in it. When you hear the word "Spirit" used in Christian circles, be reminded that this mighty Spirit is your creator God, Elohim and that Jesus himself lives in you in your spirit. Remember that as a believer in Jesus, made alive by his presence in you, you are more than just body and soul. You have been born from above and now have access to the spiritual realms where God is found. Let's work to replace the confusion that people hold about the Holy Spirit with the realization that as the Father was in the Son so the Son is in the Spirit. Now as a believer, this wondrous God has come to live in our spirits. He will comfort us in his love. He will lead us to freedom and life.

The Church

"That he might present to himself the Church..." Ephesians 5:27

When we come to the subject of the church, we come to the heart of God and the heart of the mystery. As Paul wrote to the Ephesians, "For Christ loved the church and gave himself up for her." And again, "this mystery (of oneness) is great but I am speaking of Christ and the church." Those are beautiful words. Jesus didn't just give his life to save us because his Father asked him to. No. He, too, was in love. He was in love with us.

We should not be surprised that such important ground is fiercely contested by God's enemy. The Lord said in Matthew 16, "I will build my church and the gates of the unseen shall not be prevailing against it." (Concordant Literal translation) Satan, the ruler of the gates of hell, the realms of the unseen, is a liar, a thief and a murderer. He will do all he can to undermine the work of God in building his bride, the church. Thank God, we know in advance that in Christ we are on the winning side. But the Lord has enlisted those who believe in him in this epic struggle. As members of the body of Christ we are an important part of the building that Christ called his church.

Still, there is much confusion about what the church is. To many people, the word "church" brings to mind a building where Christians with matching views about God gather on Sunday mornings. When first meeting, Christians often ask one another "Where do you go to church?" They do that because it's a convenient conversation starter. If you've been a Christian for a while, you know that based on what kind of building a person goes to on Sunday, you can generally figure out whether or not that person's relationship with God is similar to yours. Then you can decide at what level you can fellowship together. One downside to this is that such exchanges often separate believers more than they bring them together.

The world and the Lord's enemy have certainly done what they can to add to the confusion. Today we find devil worshippers calling themselves the "church of Satan" and witches using the word "church" to describe their covens. Since the word actually started out as a secular term this probably shouldn't shock us. But what is the highest and best use of this word?

What Is the Church?

The word originally used in the New Testament to describe the followers of Christ was the Greek word ecclesia. This word means "the called-out ones" and carries the meaning of an assembly. In the first century the word had no religious connotations whatsoever. In fact, the word was a political one. In Greek cities the ecclesia was called together to decide on matters affecting the community. When we consider that Jesus Christ came to earth to set up the kingdom of God, it makes perfect sense that the gathering of his people would be called the ecclesia. The meeting of the ecclesia was the government of God in action.

To further clarify its meaning, in several New Testament passages the church is called the "body of Christ." The church, then, is the assembly of those who have been called out of the world to express the reality of who Jesus is. That means that when you encounter the church as it is meant to be, you encounter Jesus. This is the fulfillment of the Lord's prayer when he said, "your kingdom come, your will be done, on earth as it is in the heavens." At her best, the church gives the world the opportunity to see Jesus in action. In essence this is the kingdom of God made visible and relevant. The church is neither religious nor secular but a new nation living under the direction of its King, Jesus Christ.

The church is also called a mystery. There is something mysterious about how the church functions in the here and now. How can an unseen

God lead a group of people? How can Jesus who sits in the heavens be the head of the church that resides on the earth? This is a mystery. Sadly, at times the church has been defined down to a set of principles or organizational structures or traditions. In so doing she has been stripped of her mysterious relationship with Jesus the Head, the One who loves to do the spontaneous and who is new every morning.

A Problem with Definitions

Modern definitions of this glorious concept can lead us in the wrong direction. Webster's Dictionary defines church as "a building for Christian worship" or "a service held in it." This definition of the word is rooted in the Greek word kyriakon which roughly meant the Lord's house. Later it became kirche in German which referred to the building where the gemeinde (the fellowship of God's people) met. From the changeover to that word it was a short step to equating the church with a building. But the church in the mind of God is not a physical building; it has never been a building; it will never be a physical building. To confine the church to an earthly building, to tie her to bricks and mortar, is to take away her mobility, her vitality and the mysterious way in which the Lord leads her.

This is not to say that believers shouldn't get together in large or small buildings. No, gathering is important and Biblical. But where believers gather is not the church, and our experience of Jesus in his body should not begin and end with events held in buildings, steepled or otherwise.

How about the original word for church: ecclesia? We see it surface today in the word "ecclesiastic." Ecclesiastic is defined in this way: "of or relating to a church as a formal and established institution;" or, "suitable for use in a church, i.e. vestments." Once again, this is a far cry from the original meaning of "called out ones" The church God birthed is not confined to formal and established institutions. It is his body, alive and full of spontaneity. It is not limited by formality. Yes, our church experience should contain awe-filled times of worship; but the extrapolation from there is not to formality and institutionalism. What could be more informal than the disciples lying around on cushions, eating a meal and listening to their Lord? That was the cradle of the church.

In our day "ecclesiastic" has been defined down to refer to vestments, or "articles of ceremonial attire and insignia worn by ecclesiastical officials as indicative of their rank." But to load the church down with rank and insignia or to define it down simply into creeds and traditions can restrict its living dynamism. While creeds and traditions can definitely be helpful in maintaining the historical connectivity and purity of the church, they exist to serve her and not the other way around.

Is there rank in the church? Scripturally and historically, we see apostles and prophets and pastors and teachers and gifts of administration and many other roles. But they do not imply rank. How is honor expressed in the church? According to the apostle Paul, "those members of the body, which we deem less honorable, on these we bestow more abundant honor; and our unseemly members come to have more abundant seemliness" (1 Corinthians 12:23). The lesser are to be honored more than the greater. There are different roles, but there's no rank.

There is a mystery about the way that Jesus leads his church that doesn't fit into organizational charts. There's a mystery in the relationship between an invisible Jesus who wants to lead and be one with his people through his Spirit and how that expresses itself. Restoring the vitality of the word "church" will take us from the stiffness of ecclesiastic vestments, rank and insignia to the newness of ecclesia and into a practical experience of God's kingdom. It is a journey worth taking.

The Church, the Complement of Jesus

When we turn to the letter to the Ephesians, we can see that the ecclesia was front and center in the mind of Paul. In the first chapter Paul prayed that the believers there would have the eyes of their hearts enlightened so they would know the hope of God's calling, the riches of the glory of God's inheritance in the saints. That's amazing! God's glorious inheritance is his people, his church. That's a high place for the ecclesia to occupy. Then Paul ended the chapter by reminding the Ephesians that following his resurrection, the Lord Jesus was raised far above all and then given as head over all things to the church, which is his body, the fullness of Him who fills all in all. That word, fullness, is a significant one. Paul used this word earlier in the letter where he wrote in verse 10 that there was a fellowship coming, suitable to the fullness of the times, the heading up of all things in Christ, things in the heavens and things on the earth."

Doing some digging, we learn that the word "fullness" came from the Greek word "complement." The complement of something is that which when joined with that something forms a perfect whole. In other words, the church is to be the complement of Christ. God in his mysterious wisdom had decided that his Son, Jesus, should have a complement, a Bride, if you will, who would be Jesus' perfect match. She would be full of Jesus and show him off to all of God's creation. He would love her with the same love that he was loved with by his Father and she would love him in return. He would be her life and she would be his expression on this earth. What a lofty role for the ecclesia to fulfill.

Amazing enough, complement is the very same word God used when he said in Genesis 2:18 "It is not good for the man to be alone; I will make a complement suitable for him." From the beginning of creation, the Father had his eye on building a bride for his Son, one who would love him and be filled with his goodness, and life. After God had paraded all the animals before Adam to be named, verse 20 says no complement was found suitable for him. That is when our mighty creator God, our Elohim, put Adam to sleep, removed a rib and from that rib, built Eve, Adam's complement and brought her to him. We know that the reality of that first bride, Eve, is the church, the ecclesia.

In Paul's wonderful prayer for the saints in Ephesians 3 he prayed that the Father would grant the believers that Christ would dwell in their hearts, that they would be rooted and grounded in love, knowing the love of Christ so that they could be filled up, completed to become the whole complement of God. That is the future we face as part of the church, the ecclesia, the fullness of the body of Christ. What a grand purpose the Lord has for us, as the church! Moving 20th century believers towards a greater understanding of the place of the church in God's thinking would be to move us toward a deeper love for others in the body of Christ and for Jesus himself. That was certainly Paul's desire in seeing the body of

Christ built up in Ephesus. And, it seems, that was a hallmark of the early Ephesians life together.

The Gathering Church

Today, our church life often consists of attending a weekly or bi-weekly event, assembling together with other believers. What then, is unique— or should be—about Christian gatherings? It is the presence of the Lord Jesus, in Spirit, in his people. The gathered church is an assembly of people where the Lord Jesus goes for fellowship. When we gather, our greatest hope and expectation is that he will be there. We will sense his presence. We will hear his voice. We will experience his love. Yes, we have likely been in Christian gatherings where that has not been our experience. But that doesn't mean we can live life just as well separated from the other parts of our Christian body.

That's why Paul told the Corinthians, "When you assemble, each one has a psalm, has a teaching, has a revelation, has a language, has an interpretation. Let all things be done for edification." (I Cor. 14:26) That sounds like a dynamic get-together. Can such freedom cause some problems? It certainly did in Corinth. But Paul's response was to encourage more participation, not less. Modern-day church practice does not often reflect what the Corinthians were used to. Most services today are primarily directed by the church staff. They are often the only type of Christian meeting the majority of believers ever experience. While such meetings have a very useful place in the life of the ecclesia, they are not the only style of Christian gathering possible.

The opportunity to know the Lord's presence in our gatherings is often heightened when people are given an opportunity to share with others what is going on in their life with Jesus. Richness comes because Jesus is expressing himself through the different members of his body. What about order? Can't such meetings get pretty crazy? Yes, they can. Especially when strong individuals insist on pushing their own agendas instead of the Lord's. But if Jesus is truly leading, then the one in charge is he who gave order to the universe and who still holds it together. Will there also be spontaneity? Yes. The Lord who created wild creatures has himself a wild streak. He is unpredictable and happily so. Should all Christian gatherings follow such a format? No. There are many ways believers can meet. But this one has been too often neglected and can add richness to our lives.

The Old Testament Sanctuary

There is a rich picture in the Old Testament that helps us understand what the real purpose of church, of ecclesia, is. That picture can be seen in the tabernacle. The Old Testament tabernacle was also called the tent of meeting. It was the place God used to dwell among his people and speak with them. God called it his sanctuary. It wasn't just used for religious purposes. Any guidance God had for his people was given there.

Here is how God introduced his people to this special place: "Then the LORD spoke to Moses, saying, Tell the sons of Israel to raise a contribution for Me, from every man whose heart moves him you shall raise my contribution…And let them construct a sanctuary for me; that I may dwell among them" (Exodus 25:1, 8). Once the tabernacle was built with those contributions of gold, silver, bronze, fine linen and so on, the Israelites continued to bring their offerings there, and God met with them. This is described in Exodus 29:42: "It shall be a continual burnt offering throughout your generations at the doorway of the tent of meeting before the LORD: where I will meet with you, to speak to you there."

The Lord's purpose in having the tabernacle set up was two directional: God would have a place on the earth to come where he could meet with his people and speak to them. God's people would have a place where they could go to hear from their God and where they could bring something for the building that he had blessed them with.

Before the tabernacle was built, the Lord had already given Moses the Ten Commandments, the requirements for living in relationship with a holy God. Those commandments, written on tablets, were put in a box called the Ark of the Covenant in the inner chamber of the tabernacle. That inner chamber was called the Holy of Holies. It was there that God's presence dwelt.

The Israelites were given the written requirements for living with God, but that was not the totality of his interaction with them. He wanted them to live by his direct instructions! Even though God gave them the Ten Commandments as a reflection of who he was and what it would take to live successfully in his presence, he also wanted to directly relate to them through the tabernacle. Notice his words, "There I will meet with you…I will speak to you about all that I will give you in commandment for the sons of Israel" (Exodus 25:22). This is the God we have. He has always wanted to be in direct relationship with those he created and loves.

The tabernacle was the place where the people of God brought their offerings. These offerings were taken to a certain place. Do you know where that place was? Over and over again in Exodus and Leviticus we read that the people were to bring their offerings to the door of the tabernacle. They were also to congregate there when the Lord had something to say to them. The door holds special significance for us in this regard. The burnt offerings (Exodus 40:6), the sin offerings (Leviticus 7:2), the peace offerings (Numbers 6:18), the guilt offerings (Leviticus 19:21) and the grain offerings (Exodus 29:41) were all to be brought to the door of the tabernacle for presentation to the priests and through them to God.

Standing at the Door

Consider these fascinating verses in Exodus 33:7-11: "Now Moses used to take the tent and pitch it outside the camp, a good distance from the camp, and he called it the tent of meeting. And everyone who sought the LORD would go out to the tent of meeting which was outside the camp And it came about, whenever Moses went out to the tent, that all the people would arise and stand, each at the entrance of his tent, and gaze after Moses until he entered the tent. Whenever Moses entered the tent, the pillar of cloud would descend and stand at the entrance of the tent; and the LORD would speak with Moses. When all the people saw the pillar of cloud standing at the entrance of the tent, all the people would arise and worship each at the entrance of his tent. Thus the LORD used to speak to Moses face to face, just as a man speaks to his friend."

At the time this tent of meeting was set up, the Lord was angry with the Israelites. Why was that? While Moses was up on the mountain getting instructions from God on how the Israelites were to live, the people got impatient, not knowing what Moses was up to or if he was even still alive. Believing they needed some kind of god for protection, they demanded that Aaron make them one. Gathering together golden earrings, he had a golden calf constructed. Naturally, when Moses came down out of the presence of the living God, he was furious with the people. He had the calf demolished and God caused a plague to fall on the idol worshipping people. Nonetheless, God still wanted to dwell among his people. So Moses took this tent and set it up outside the camp and called it the tent of meeting.

Everyone who sought the Lord would go out to the tent of meeting. God made himself available to them there. This is what made the Israelites unique in all the earth. God didn't interact with the Philistines or the Canaanites or the Amalekites or the Amorites or any of the other people dwelling in that area. He dwelt with the Israelites and his place of dwelling among them was the sanctuary, the tent of meeting.

Moses and his servant Joshua were the only ones who actually got to go into the tent. When Moses went out to that tent, all of the Israelites watched him go. Not only that, whenever Moses went out to the tent, all the men would also go somewhere. They went to the doorway of their own tents. In the culture of the day, the man represented his household, so this picture represents all of God's people. The men would arise and stand at the door of their tents. Whenever Moses entered the tent, a cloud came down and God would come to meet and speak with Moses. What an experience! Picture your God, waiting for Moses to come out to the tent so he could meet with him and they could talk, face to face as a man would talk to his friend. Meanwhile, all the men of Israel would arise and worship, each at the doorway to his tent. The whole nation of Israel was involved in this picture of God having fellowship with his people.

At that time Moses went in and met with God face to face. But can you see the symbolism as all those men stood in their doorways, worshipping as well. No doubt they stood there wondering what it was like inside, wishing they, too, could spend time with God as they would with a friend.

God wanted to be friends with Moses? Yes. In fact our God invented the idea of friendship. The amazing truth is that just as God was friends with Moses and enjoyed spending time with him, he feels the same way toward you. Do you need a friend? There is none better than Jesus. In the friendship of Moses and his God, we have a beautiful picture of what gathering in the tent of meeting might look like.

But does that have something to do with the church? Yes! The day has come when all the people of God can enter that tent of meeting and know him, face to face, and talk with him as a man talks with his friend. Here's how the apostle John described meeting with the living God: "What was from the beginning, what we have heard, what we have seen with our eyes, what we beheld and our hands handled… what we have seen and heard we proclaim to you also, so that you also may have fellowship with us; and indeed our fellowship is with the Father, and with his Son Jesus Christ." (I John 1: 1-3) That is very personal! Thank God, we, too, have been invited into the tent of meeting to be friends with the Father and the Son.

Paul said the same thing when he wrote, "God is faithful, through whom you were called into fellowship with his Son, Jesus Christ our Lord" (I Corinthians 1:9). If the word fellowship has a stuffy, religious connotation for you, replace it with the word friendship. Your God, Yahweh Elohim, will not mind at all. He made it clear that all God's people were included in this wonderful friendship when he said, "For you are all sons of God through faith in Christ Jesus. For all of you who were baptized into Christ have clothed yourselves with Christ. There is neither Jew nor Greek, there is neither slave nor free man, there is neither male nor female; for you are all one in Christ Jesus" (Galatians 3:26-28). Another beautiful Bible verse says this, "For God was in Christ, reconciling the world the world to Himself, not counting their sins against them." ((2 Corinthians 5:19) The dictionary definition for reconcile is "to restore friendship." This makes perfect sense given our earlier discussion of the meaning of the Lord's name Yahweh. In Christ we have moved from Sie to Du with our heavenly Father. May it be so in our experience.

From this we know that the church is the body of God's people living in friendship and love with him. We are the place where God enjoys hanging out. Through Jesus, we have the kind of access to God that the High Priest of the tabernacle could only have dreamed about. The High Priest could only enter into the copy of the true tabernacle. We enter into our heavenly Father's very presence. When we gather together, we can share what we have experienced in being with our Lord and through his activity in our lives. That will include real-life struggles, victories, prayers, praises, sorrows and songs. Encouraged by the realness of Christ in our midst, we can then go out to engage a hurting world with his love.

A Kingdom of Priests

When God first brought the Israelites out of Egypt, he wanted a whole nation of priests. Exodus 19:5 says, "Now then, if you will indeed obey my voice and keep my covenant, then you shall be my own possession among all the peoples…and you shall be to me a kingdom of priests and a holy nation." But under the old covenant God singled out one family (Aaron's) of the tribe of Levi to carry out the duties of the priesthood. Out of that tribe only the High Priest could actually enter the Holy of Holies where God dwelt. Jesus Christ changed all that. He did not come from the tribe of Levi but from the tribe of Judah. He was the first of a new order of priests As Peter wrote in his first letter to the church scattered across Asia, "And coming to him as to a living stone which has been rejected by men, but choice and precious in the sight of God, you also, as living stones, are being built up as a spiritual house for a holy priesthood, to offer up spiritual sacrifices acceptable to God through Jesus Christ… you are a chosen race, a royal priesthood, a holy nation, a people for God's own possession, so that you may proclaim the excellencies of him who has called you out of darkness into his marvelous light." (I Peter 2:4, 11)

The church was not designed to be an assembly of people where just one or a few people who have been in the presence of God describe what that is like while everyone else watches and worships as best they can. If that is all we have, we are much like those Israelites standing at their tents hoping Moses was enjoying his time with God. The New Testament church is a body of people who all know God, report how near he is and together express his will on the earth. This can take many forms including meeting for worship, sharing in each other's hard times, reaching out to the poor, caring for the sick, gathering for teaching, meeting for coffee or a beer, going on adventures together, sharing meals, celebrating kingdom life through the Lord's Supper and so forth. There is wonderful variety in the ways in which the body of Christ builds itself up.

Everyone Has a Part

The reality of the church being a corporate people expressing the richness of God's goodness is reinforced in other Old Testament passages. We have already cited God's instructions for how the tabernacle was to be built where Exodus 25 says, "from every man whose heart moves him you shall raise my contribution." Everyone with a willing heart was asked to contribute. Everyone had something they could give.

Consider these verses:

Exodus 35:5: "Take from among you a contribution to the LORD; whoever is of a willing heart, let him bring it as the LORD'S contribution: gold, silver, and bronze."

Exodus 35:29: "The Israelites, all the men and women, whose heart moved them to bring material for all the work, which the LORD had commanded through Moses to be done, brought a freewill offering to the LORD."

Exodus 36:5: "and they said to Moses, 'The people are bringing much more than enough for the construction work which the LORD commanded us to perform.'"

God builds his church by stirring up the hearts of those who love him to offer what they can to build up his body. When he does that, there is more than enough to accomplish what God wants. This has been going on for the past 2000 years and continues today. Jesus said, "I will build my church" and that is exactly what he is doing. In this regard we should not consider only that which is done by those in full-time Christian service as the building work of God. Such thinking leaves many of God's people with a seat on the sidelines watching and evaluating the performance of others. This is never the way the church has best expressed its vitality.

Paul laid that out in Ephesians 4:11-12: "He gave some as apostles, and some as prophets, and some as evangelists, and some as pastors and teachers, for the equipping of the saints for the work of service, to the building up of the body of Christ." This verse says that while some equip the greater body of Christ (the saints, the holy ones, you and me), through leadership and teaching we are all involved in the work of building up the body. The effective building up of the body doesn't happen only during organized gatherings. It occurs in the trenches of daily life; one sister encouraging another, a brother upholding another, friends weeping with friends during life's dark hours and rejoicing with them when the sun breaks through. These are places where lasting building occurs.

We need those who share the wonders of Christ and the greatness of his plan with the people of God. Without a vision the people lose heart. As Paul said in verses 15 and 16 of Ephesians 4, "we are to grow up in all aspects into him who is the head, even Christ, from whom the whole body, being fitted and held together by that which every joint supplies, according to the proper working of each individual part, causes the growth of the body for the building up of itself in love." This is the whole body of Christ energized by his life flow, giving what they have, working together and falling in love with one another and their Lord in the process. This is worth the cost that may be involved. God has given his people the gifts needed to see the building built. Because that is true, we need one another.

The Tabernacle Moves into the House

The tabernacle was God's dwelling place among his people as they moved across the wilderness. But when they got into the Promised Land, that arrangement changed. God established a permanent place where his Name would dwell and where the Israelites would come to gather before him. Here's what Deuteronomy 12:5 says: "But you shall seek the Lord at the place which the LORD your God shall choose to establish his name there for his dwelling, and there shall you come:"

II Chronicles 6:6 shows where this place is: "But I have chosen Jerusalem that my name might be there." When the Israelites entered the

Promised Land, Jerusalem was established as the place where God's Name would be honored, where the temple was built to be God's sanctuary. II Chronicles 7:1 describes what happened when the temple was finished: "Now when Solomon had finished praying, fire came down from heaven, and consumed the burnt offering and the sacrifices; and the glory of the Lord filled the house. And the priests could not enter into the house of the Lord, because the glory of the Lord had filled the Lord's house."

As God's plan moved from the temporary to the permanent in the Old Testament, the tabernacle became the temple. The temple was referred to most often as the house of God. The amazing thing is that God actually filled that house with his presence and glory. There was a place on earth, in Jerusalem, where God dwelt and from which he wanted to lead his people.

In the New Testament, the apostles Paul and Peter, as well as the writer of Hebrews, referred to the church as the dwelling of God. This was now the place on earth where God's presence and glory would be seen. While the term "house of God" is commonly used in our day to refer to a building where religious people gather, in God's mind his house is not a building made of brick or stone but one made of living stones filled with the Lord Jesus. As Paul wrote to the Corinthians, "For we are God's fellow workers; you are God's field, God's building"

The Tabernacle Becomes Real

When the Lord Jesus arrived on earth, he came as the true tabernacle of God. John described his coming in this way: "The Word became flesh and dwelt (literally, tabernacled) among us; and we beheld his glory, glory as of the only begotten from the Father, full of grace and truth." When Jesus Christ came to earth, the beginning of God's plan to fully indwell his creation became a reality.

One day Jesus walked with his disciples past the temple in Jerusalem. His disciples were impressed. "Wow, what a building, what an incredible temple!" they said. Jesus' response was amazing: "Tear this temple down and in three days I will raise it again." From Jesus' perspective, the real house of God was not contained in a man-made building, no matter how beautiful it was. He was the first stone of the building God wanted to live in. Through the tearing down of his physical body we too would become part of that house.

How does that happen? Jesus Christ was crucified, resurrected, glorified, and then returned to his disciples and breathed his Spirit into them in the upper room. Then on Pentecost, the Holy Spirit anointed all the followers of Christ and the ecclesia, the church, the body of Christ, was fully born.

Let's consider what's happening. In the Old Testament the temporary tabernacle expanded into the temple. But these were only shadows or pictures of what was to come. In the New Testament the tabernacling Christ, limited by human flesh, expanded into the house of God by indwelling believers with his Holy Spirit. That's what Peter was talking about when he wrote in I Peter 2:4, "Coming to Jesus as to a living stone, rejected by men, but chosen and precious in the sight of God, you also, as living stones, are being built up as a spiritual house, for a holy priesthood, to offer up spiritual sacrifices, acceptable to God through Jesus Christ."

Paul echoed this in Ephesians 2:20-22 where he wrote, "Christ Jesus himself being the chief corner stone; in whom the whole building being fitly framed together is growing into a holy temple in the Lord: In whom you also are being built together into a dwelling of God in the Spirit." This is the church, vital, alive and growing into a dwelling of God in the Spirit. This is the church that you and I were added to when we became followers of the Lord Jesus.

The Source of Life

How does this church get built? From where does it derive its energy, its direction and its unity? The answer is clear from our Old Testament pictures. God first met in a tent with his friend Moses to give guidance to his people. Then he moved into the temporary Holy of Holies in the tabernacle and from there into the temple. From that holy place he gave direction to his people. But only one high priest could go into the Holy of Holies, and that was once a year. The best an Israelite in the wilderness could do was stand at his tent door and watch while Moses fellowshipped with God. The best an Israelite in the Promised Land could do was go to Jerusalem three times a year and bring an offering to the priest.

Where is the Holy of Holies today? It is still in the heart of the temple. We who are believers in Christ are the temple! In each of us there is a sacred place called our spirit where Christ dwells. The writer of Hebrews put it this way in Hebrews 10:10: "By this will, we have been sanctified through the offering of the body of Jesus Christ once for all." And again in verse 14, "For by one offering he has perfected for all time those that are sanctified." The word "sanctified" is a very important one. This is the same word from which the word "sanctuary" comes. There is a connection between the sanctuary and our being sanctified. We have been set apart, called out from the kingdom of darkness, to be the sanctuary of the living God, to be his dwelling place. That is glorious!

This is what the Lord Jesus was talking about in John 17:22-23 when he said, "The glory which you have given me, I have given to them, that they may be one, just as we are one, I in them and you in Me that they may be perfected in unity." Through our fellowship with the Christ within us, we enter the presence of our God and Father. He is in us and we are in him. As we individually and corporately fellowship with him and follow his voice, he builds us together into his dwelling. Because he lives in us, we get to see him in action. There was nothing more invigorating (and dangerous) in first century Palestine than to hang out with Jesus Christ. The same is true today.

Paul wrote to the Corinthians, "Don't you know that you are a sanctuary of God and the spirit of God dwells in you?" Who would you rather be, one of those Israelites standing at their tent door worshipping and wishing they could know what was going on in there with Moses, or a believer in the twenty-first century who can go into your inner room and fellowship with your loving Father? He is in us to speak to us, to meet with us, to fellowship with us, to love us, to talk to us face to face as we talk to a friend. This is the life blood of ecclesia. This is the source and well-spring of the church. Thank God, the Old Testament pictures are gone and the reality has come.

Three Aspects of the Church

The Bible describes the church in three ways. There is the church local. That is the fellowship of believers found in a specific geographical location. Paul refers to the "church of God which is at Corinth," "the churches of Galatia," "the church of the Thessalonians," and so forth. That church could meet in homes, as they did in the home of Nymphas in Laodicea, the house of Philemon in Colosse, and the home of Priscilla and Aquila in Rome. Or it could meet at a central place like Solomon's Porch in Jerusalem. The point is that all of the believers in a location were part of the same church, the same body of Christ. Did they all meet together all the time? Not necessarily. Were all the meetings the same? Not likely. Surely they met for teaching, for meals, for prayer, and for hanging out. But wherever they met and however they met, all the believers were still part of the same church.

But Which Structure is the Right One?

How various bodies of believers choose to organize themselves is a subject involving almost unlimited diversity of thought and practice. Are the Orthodox faiths the correct ones? How about the house church way of gathering? Isn't that the most Biblical? How about all those in between? We can choose from Pentecostals to Methodists to Anglicans to Baptists to Brethren and on and on. Some say organizational authority and church direction should not be local, but centralized in a place like New York, London, Rome, or Istanbul. Such a view makes other believers' hair stand on end. Having had 2000 years to think about it, you'd think we'd have arrived at some clarity on the subject. Sadly not. Christianity currently includes some 33,000 different identifiable church bodies.

Personally, I came to Christ in the late 1960's when the Lord was moving in a large-scale way both inside and outside of traditional denominational church structures. The believers I gathered with met both in homes and in larger venues for teaching and corporate worship and sharing. Many of the meetings were wonderfully full of the Lord's presence and our daily lives included much interaction with one another. But movements of God tend to be just that and if we find ourselves in one, we should enjoy them while they last. New seasons come and we are to follow the Lord where he is going. As a result, my family and I have attended a variety of Christian fellowships over the years. All have contributed something to us and hopefully the contribution has gone the other way as well. Some readers may relate to that experience. Others may have had the experience of being in the same community of believers their whole Christian life.

The best situation for all of us when it comes to connecting with believers is to be part of a fellowship where the life of Christ is shared, where God the Father has the chance to make himself known in our lives, and where the Spirit is free to move. Under such conditions, your heart will draw you into deeper connectedness with those people. Your church experience will not be a chore but an integral part of healthy living.

At the same time, keep your heart open to other believers who hold a different view of how the church is structured than you do. Being narrow minded about our church affiliation only serves to further divide the Lord's body in unnecessary ways. All of this is not to say that life together might not get messy. It will. We all know that family life has its intense, stressful times. Experiencing the body life that Christ offers us is no different. But like healthy family life, the fruit of life together is love that endures. This is a great gift of God to us. There are few you will come to value more.

The Church Universal and Historical

Secondly there is the church universal. This is the body of Christ spread all over the world, through which the Lord is doing his kingdom work. It is a great encouragement to be aware of, and in some measure connected to, the work God is doing around the world. It is especially important that we in the West, who experience little of suffering or opposition for our faith, have some idea of what our fellow believers are suffering for the Name of Christ in foreign lands. Such knowledge is both humbling and stirring.

Thirdly, there is the church timeless. This is the body of Christ across the ages, saved by the blood of the Lamb, made up of all whose names are recorded in the Lamb's book of Life. This is the church referred to by Paul in Ephesians 5:25-27 when he wrote, "Husbands, love your wives, just as Christ also loved the church, and gave himself up for her; That he might sanctify her having cleansed her by the washing of water by the word, that he might present to himself the church in all her glory, having no spot, or wrinkle, or any such thing; but that she should be holy and blameless."

We see that church, that glorious assembly of God's people, again in Revelation 21:2 where the apostle John writes, "And I saw the holy city, new Jerusalem, coming down out of heaven from God, made ready as a bride adorned for her husband." Now pay attention to the next verse: "And I heard a loud voice from the throne saying, Behold, the tabernacle of God is among men, and he shall dwell among them, and they shall be his people, and God himself shall be among them."

This is the ultimate purpose of God in this universe: to dwell with and in his people. He wants us to have a foretaste of that holy city now through the body of Christ, the church. It is through the church that the Lord makes his love and wisdom known; it is through the church that he defeats his enemy. It is through the church that the nations catch a glimpse of the greatness of our God. Our invitation is to practice and encourage the free movement of Christ in his people so that more of him can be expressed on this earth and his enemy can be crushed.

The Church or the Kingdom?

How about the church and the kingdom? Is there one of those we should emphasize? As someone who focused on the church for close to 30 years of my Christian life, I can tell you it is better to be part of the church and stand for the kingdom. Jesus preached the kingdom and built the church. Paul did likewise. I believe it is the better part of wisdom to do the same. For example, do we baptize new believers into a church body or into the kingdom? John the Baptist immersed people in water to prepare them for kingdom living, not church membership. After Jesus was baptized, he went everywhere preaching the kingdom of God. It is that kingdom which carries on into eternity.

In Corinth when believers looked to their source of baptism for their spiritual identity, the result was division. While the church is primarily local and tied to time and space, the kingdom is global and eternal. The reality is that the church serves the kingdom, not the other way around. If we are having a vital experience of the body of Christ, we are living out the rule of God's kingdom. We are seeing that kingdom made practical in our lives. The exaltation of Jesus Christ and his work at the cross is our highest and best point of focus. As Paul put it so beautifully in Philippians 3:3: "For we are the real circumcision (i.e. the real people of God) who worship in the Spirit and glory in Christ Jesus and put no confidence in the flesh." On that ground we can all meet together.

Closing Thoughts

When you hear the word "church," realize that the church is not a physical building but the body of people who are following Christ. The church is not something that can be experienced only on Sundays but happens when the Lord's people are linked together in the love of God and unite to express his will on the earth. The Lord said, "I will build my church and the gates of hell will not overpower it." Here he was talking about those unseen forces of darkness that fight to keep Jesus from being known. In that light, let's ask the Lord to work anew in his church to bring beauty, vitality and newness to his people. In this way the earth will be blessed and many can know the goodness of his presence. The Lord must build if we are to have newness in our relationship with him and other believers. But he has invited us to labor with him in this work. We are the apple of his eye and his partner in defeating our common foe. After all, we are his body, the church.

The Cross

**"But may it never be that I should boast, except
in the cross of our Lord Jesus Christ"**

The first century crucifixion of Jesus Christ was one of the pivotal events
of human history. Because of Christ's death there, God was able to fulfill
his eternal plan of building a Bride for his Son. Your destiny and mine will
be decided by our acceptance of what God accomplished there through
Jesus Christ. Jesus' death on the cross and his subsequent resurrection
set him apart from every other person, prophet or religious leader. While
every religion accepts Jesus in some form or other, only Christianity exalts
Christ and him crucified. Only a crucified Jesus takes care of the problem
of sin that impacts the human race. As the writer of Hebrews put it, "And
according to the Law...all things are cleansed with blood, and without
shedding of blood there is no forgiveness" (Hebrews 9:22).

For many Christians, the mention of the cross as it relates to our lives
can be intimidating. We are thankful for the cross, because we know that
Christ's death there enabled us to be forgiven for our sin. But when we
encounter verses like those in Mark 8:34-35 where Jesus says, "If anyone
wishes to come after me, he must deny himself, and take up his cross and
follow me," we get nervous. We are not sure what the implications are of
taking up our cross. Those implications can be scary. We may think we
are facing a life of denying much of what we enjoy. God's enemy feeds
into our insecurity by presenting to us the image of a life lived in dull
monotony, where we are at the mercy of a strict God waiting to punish us

whenever we get out of line. But such thoughts have nothing to do with what Jesus did at the cross.

What propelled God to send his Son to the cross? It was his love. God so loved the world that he gave his only begotten Son. Love was behind the activity of the cross in the life of Christ. Likewise, love is behind the daily crosses that God sends us to bear. Jesus was secure in his Father's love. He knew the glory that was waiting for him (and us) on the other side of that cross. That's why he could follow his Father wherever the Father led him, even to his death. Because of that death the love of God and the eternal desire he had for believers in Christ —making them part of his own family—is now ours to experience through faith in Jesus.

Take Up Your Cross and Follow Me

The Lord talked about the cross with his disciples before the crucifixion. He wanted them to know in advance that while the cross would be the instrument of his death, its work would benefit those who followed him. Here is the story: "And Jesus began to teach them that the Son of Man must suffer many things and be rejected by the elders and the chief priests and the scribes, and be killed, and after three days, rise again. And he was stating the matter plainly. And Peter took him aside and began to rebuke him. But turning around and seeing his disciples, he rebuked Peter and said, 'Get behind me, Satan; for you are not setting your mind on God's interests, but man's.' And he summoned the crowd with his disciples, and said to them, 'If anyone wishes to come after me, he must deny himself, and take up his cross and follow me. For whoever wishes to save his life will lose it, but whoever loses his life for my sake and the gospel's will save it. For what does it profit a man to gain the whole world, and forfeit his soul?'" (Mark 8:31-36).

Jesus made it plain that to fulfill his purpose he would have to suffer many things, including rejection and death. In doing so, he described himself as the Son of Man. This suffering was not his because he was the Son of God. No, this suffering was because he was human.

As such, he undertook this suffering on behalf of all humanity. Peter's reaction was startling. He took Jesus aside and began to rebuke him. This tells us something about the approachableness and humility of the Lord Jesus. The creator of the universe, the son of God, the miracle worker, was so humble that Peter, a fisherman, felt the freedom to pull him aside and rebuke him. Evidently Jesus did not "lord it over" his followers or strike fear into their hearts. Thank God, he didn't then and he doesn't now.

We could look down on Peter. We could criticize him for his stupidity. But if we had been in his position, we might have done the same thing. Peter didn't like where Jesus was going with all this talk of suffering and death, especially death by crucifixion. This was the most shameful of deaths, reserved for the worst criminals. From Peter's view things were going pretty well. Yes, there was the occasional dust-up. But Jesus was getting famous. Lots of people were following him. People were getting fed, even healed. And, perhaps best of all, Peter was in Jesus' inner circle. Why mess it up by talking about rejection and death?

It's reasonable to think that Peter was looking down the road at what might happen to Jesus' followers if Jesus were killed. Not only would Peter's hopes of future glory be dashed, but he might be in actual danger. Obviously, the part about being raised up in three days hadn't sunk in very far. But we can hardly blame Peter for that. He did not have much experience with seeing someone who had been brutally murdered come back to life.

But Jesus was not humored by Peter's rebuke. Nor did he make any attempt to sugar-coat his response: "Get behind Me, Satan; for you are not setting your mind on God's interests, but man's." In this case, man's interests were maintaining the status quo—not rocking the boat, self-preservation. Man's interests did not include the admission that a sacrificial death was needed to cover sin. Man's interests included the protection of the soul and staying away from any denial of the self. All of these things reflected Satan's interests as well, allowing him to retain his control over a sinful humanity.

God is Interested in Us

But God's interests were far different. God was interested in redeeming the sinful human race. He was interested in making his creation whole. He wanted to crush his enemy and see his son Jesus magnified. God loved his creation and knew that to go on with the status quo would result in his precious creation perishing, lost in sin. As John 3:16 reminds us, "For God so loved the world that he gave his only begotten son that whoever believes in him should not perish but have eternal life." If Jesus had given in to Peter's rebuke, the result would have been Peter's perishing. Peter didn't know that. He didn't know that the status quo was that the enemy had taken control of mankind. He didn't know that the end of all things for man was eternal death.

But God the Father knew it. His interests centered on saving mankind from that fate. His interest wasn't in punishment. His interest was in redemption. But God's enemy, Satan, had infiltrated man's thinking. The enemy had no desire to see his captives released. Jesus knew where Peter's message was coming from and directly addressed the source. With his words, "Get behind me, Satan," Jesus let his enemy know that nothing could stop him from ending Satan's tyrannical reign over mankind.

Satan also knew that Jesus' obedience to the Father was his greatest obstacle in overcoming the power that Jesus had over him. If Jesus would abandon the path of obedience that he was on, Satan would once again triumph over man as he had in the Garden of Eden. But Jesus was not swayed. He let his followers know that not only was his path leading him to the cross, but it would lead them there as well. There the power of Satan would be crushed.

When Jesus invited his followers to follow him, he was fully aware that the journey would not end at the cross. On the other side of the cross Jesus was going back to his Father, to be seated in heavenly places. As Paul wrote, "These are in accordance with the working of the strength of God's might, which he brought about in Christ, when he raised him from the dead and seated him at his right hand in the heavenly places" (Ephesians 1:19-20). Jesus was fully confident of that when he said, "If anyone wants to come after me, let him take up his cross and follow me."

He sat down at the right hand of God. That's where he was going, and we have been invited to go there with him. The road to that heavenly seat goes through the cross.

Jesus made it clear that not only would forgiveness of sin be given to those who follow him, but the receiving of a new life, as well. That's why he said in Mark 8, "whoever wishes to save his life shall lose it, but whoever loses his life for my sake and the gospel's will save it." The literal word for "lose" in that passage is "destroy." Jesus knew that he was the only solution for the power of death that had infected man. That's why he said, "I am the way, the truth and the life, no one comes to the Father but through me." If we are not in Christ, we are in the realm of his enemy, Satan. The enemy's purpose for man is destruction. Following Jesus, on the other hand, leads to life eternal.

The Benefits Multiply

It's significant that Jesus said, "For my sake and the gospel's." We are not just taking up our cross for Jesus' sake. There is another reason for us to deny ourselves and follow Christ. It is not just for him, nor is it just for us personally. The Lord is building a body, a kingdom, a city, and a bride. This is the full gospel. When we take up our cross and follow Jesus, the whole building benefits. When we lay down our egos, our pride, our selfishness, and our destructive behaviors to choose Jesus, the body of Christ is strengthened.

Peter did not initially understand why Jesus needed to die on his behalf. But as he later wrote to believers everywhere, "he himself bore our sins in his body on the cross, so that we might die to sin and live to righteousness; for by his wounds you were healed" (1 Peter 2:24).

God's will, as revealed in John 3:16, is that we would not perish but have eternal life. That life would be transmitted to us by Jesus the life giving Spirit. As Peter put it, "For Christ also died for sins once for all, the just for the unjust, so that he might bring us to God, having been put to death in the flesh, but made alive in the Spirit" (1 Peter 3:18). At the cross our Lord was released as the Spirit to wipe our sins away and bring us into the presence of his Father.

The Cross and the Building

Luke 14 tells the story of Jesus being followed by huge multitudes. Up until then, he had healed people, turned water into wine, mass-produced food, driven out demons and spoken with authority. If he were interested in establishing an earthly kingdom, this would be the time to rally the forces. But instead Jesus chose to drive home the message of the cross.

As the crowds pressed in on him, Jesus yelled out, "If anyone comes to me, and does not hate his own father and mother and wife and children and brothers and sisters, yes, and even his own life, he cannot be my disciple. Whoever does not carry his own cross and come after me cannot be my disciple."

Ouch.

Hate my father, hate my mother, carry a cross? Those were hard words to swallow. What about more free food? What about getting rid of the oppressive Roman government? But let's not overlook Jesus' opening words…"if anyone comes to me." From God's perspective this is what it's all about: coming to Jesus. Do you want to come to him? Do you want to hang out with him? This is the central question regarding the Lord Jesus. Being with him makes whatever follows worthwhile. As Jesus put it before going to that cross, "Father, I desire that they also, whom you have given me, be with me where I am, so that they may see my glory which you have given me, for you loved me before the foundation of the world" (John 17:24). The purpose of the cross is getting us to where Jesus is so that we can experience life with him. According to Jesus, that includes seeing something glorious. That sounds promising.

Considering what Jesus said, it is fair to consider if there is any indication that Jesus despised his mother. The evidence shows otherwise. In fact, as he hung dying on the cross, Jesus made sure his mother would be cared for. And there is certainly no New Testament instruction that encourages husbands to hate their wives. Just the opposite is true. Paul exhorted the Ephesian believers to love their wives, as Christ loved the church, and gave himself up for it. So obviously, Jesus was saying something deeper here than his words imply. Some say that Jesus was trying to draw a comparison for us. The idea is that our love for Jesus is to be so great that, in contrast, our love for those closest to us seems like hate. But if we are honest with ourselves we have to say that even that is not the case. Most of us cannot honestly say that we love Jesus so much that our feelings for our parents, spouses and children seem like hate. I know I can't.

So what's the point? My conclusion is that what Jesus was asking here is impossible. Under the conditions Jesus sets forth, it is impossible for us to be his disciples. While that may seem shocking, it shouldn't be. Jesus was letting that crowd know that something more than just their good intentions or a passing interest in the things of God were necessary to follow him; there would be a cost involved. They could not do it on their own. They would need the power of a greater life.

Jesus spelled out the cost in his following words: "For which one of you when he wants to build a tower does not first sit down and calculate the costs to see if he has enough to complete it? Otherwise when he has laid a foundation and is not able to finish, all who observe him begin to ridicule him saying, this man began to build and was not able to finish." (Luke 14:28-30). When God started to build his kingdom on earth, Jesus Christ was the cornerstone of that building. When Jesus was in Jerusalem, he walked past the temple with his disciples. The disciples were amazed by its beautiful stones and buildings. After hearing their words of praise for the physical building, Jesus made the preposterous statement that if the temple were destroyed, in three days he would raise it up. These words show that he was on a mission to build the real house of God.

Jesus' words about the temple evidently were spread all over town. Surely there was some snickering going on as the rumor spread. Perhaps even his own disciples thought he had gone too far this time. Was Jesus going to lead an insurrection that involved tearing down the precious temple? How could anyone build such a glorious building in three days? Little did his detractors know how great that building would become. When Jesus stood trial before the Jewish authorities, these words were thrown back in his face. Accusers stood before him and testified, "This man stated, 'I am able to destroy the temple of God and to rebuild it in three days'" (Matthew 26:61). Later on, when Jesus hung on the cross, his words were once again used to taunt and humiliate him. "Those passing by were hurling abuse at him, wagging their heads and saying,

'You who are going to destroy the temple and rebuild it in three days, save yourself! If you are the Son of God, come down from the cross.' In the same way the chief priests also, along with the scribes and elders, were mocking him and saying, he saved others; he cannot save himself." (Matthew 27:39-42)

In Luke 14 Jesus warned those who followed him that the day would come when those who built for his kingdom would be accused of not having counted the cost; that they would be ridiculed for not being able to finish what they had started. His words came true in his own life. As Jesus hung on the cross, to the world it certainly seemed as if he did not finish what he had come to start. After all, there he hung dying, with no one to save him. But Jesus had counted the cost. He knew that it would cost him everything to bring his Father's plan to successful completion. He had complete faith that his Father would raise him up again by the power of his indestructible life. Jesus Christ needed the help of the eternal life of his Father to complete this building. As Peter declared at Pentecost, "But God raised him up again, putting an end to the agony of death, since it was impossible for him to be held in its power." (Acts 2:24)

Just as Jesus Christ needed the life of his Father to carry out his part of the building, you and I need the same. If we follow Jesus, we can be sure that days will come when we feel we cannot finish what we've started, that being a Christian requires more than we can give. At such times our thoughts will testify against us, accusing us of not having what it takes to live the Christian life at the level Jesus seemingly demands. But if we did have what it takes to live the Christian life, we wouldn't have needed the cross. I can count the cost of being a believer all day long, but in the end there is only one way I can do it. That is through the life of the Lord Jesus Christ living in me, cleansing me from sin and empowering me with his life. That is the message of the cross. On our own, we do not have what it takes to live as Christians. Simply put, we need Jesus. In moments of doubt God is closer than we can know, waiting to encourage us in our desperation that he is the One who has called us and he is the One who perfects the work that he has begun in us. We need the power of a resurrected Christ. Thank God, his life was made available to us through the cross.

The Cross Makes Us Salty

Jesus went on to let the crowd know what his expectations were. He said, "Or what king, when he sets out to meet another king in battle, will not first sit down and take counsel whether he is strong enough with ten thousand men to encounter the one coming against him with twenty thousand? Or else, while the other is still far away, he sends a delegation and asks for terms of peace. So therefore, none of you can be my disciple who does not give up all his own possessions. Therefore, salt is good; but if even salt has become tasteless, with what will it be seasoned? It is useless either for the soil or for the manure pile; it is thrown out. He who has ears to hear, let him hear" (Luke 14:31-35).

In this passage the Lord groups going out to war, giving up our possessions and the value of salt in a provocative way. These illustrations followed the Lord's admonition that those wanting to be his disciples had to pick up their cross and follow him.

Consider the illustration of the kings. A king with ten thousand men is about to encounter a king with twenty thousand men who is steadily moving into his territory. Those are not good odds for the first king. The implication is that if he is smart, he will send out a delegation to ask for terms of peace and to find out what it will cost him to enjoy that peace.

Here's what I take from this. The king with the greater strength is Jesus. He is the king of glory who has come to conquer us with his love. The lesser king is me (and you). We're the ones Jesus wants to rule over. To our eternal gain, he is stronger, and he will win this battle. We see him coming and if we're smart, we're thinking, "Whoa, I'd better ask for peace. Lord, what is it going to take to have peace with you?" Jesus' response is all-consuming.

"I want everything you have!"

Jesus' terms of peace are that he wants everything! No matter how much or how little you may think you have, he wants it all! It was as if Jesus put up a sign that said, "Follow me at your own risk." This is the gospel. Imagine the thoughts that must have swept through that crowd. Those masses following Jesus to see what they might get next finally got to see the price tag. He was demanding everything from them.

Jesus wants everything we've got. That doesn't mean he wants us to be poor. No, not at all. In fact, He wants us to reach our highest potential and then turn it all over to him, including our lives. He wants us to come to him and say, "Okay, Lord, you can have it all! Use it any way you see fit." That's a challenge worth responding to. Are we talking here about possessions? Yes. Are we talking about our careers? Yes. Are we talking about our families? Yes. He wants it all.

That doesn't mean that the Lord's highest purpose is for you and me to sell everything and go overseas to be missionaries. Many people have gotten the message that to follow Christ at the most committed level means they will become some type of minister or missionary, or that God places a higher value on that which is called "Christian service." God does ask some people to do such things, but that message is not correct. God does not place a higher value on one kind of vocation over another. No, God wants you to live for him right where you are, with the talents and interests he's given you, in the midst of a society that has little idea of what it means to be truly free.

My wife and I have given up everything we own several times. We once lived in a situation where for several years we pooled all our possessions with other believers. That lifestyle had certain joys to it but it was also difficult. We've lived overseas, and we've moved across the United States four times. We know what it's like to pinch pennies. But we have also lived in some of the world's most beautiful locations. Our four children all went to excellent universities. We have the blessed joy of living near three of them and their families. We own a nice home and have decent cars. But the Lord might ask us to leave those possessions behind and start somewhere new tomorrow. We would have a choice to make. Do we want to follow him into new adventures of faith, or do we want to camp where we are?

He could ask for it. He's done it before; he might do it again. But following Jesus is not about having things or not having things. It's about saying Yes, Lord. Do we want to make peace with him? He knows that the greatest peace comes when all that we have is turned over to him. Is this not the greatest lesson that we learn from the Lord Jesus when he prayed in the garden, "Not my will but yours be done."

That prayer cost him literally everything. But it also opened the door to boundless blessing for those who would receive him after his death and resurrection.

Following the parable about the kings, Jesus moved on to talk about salt. "Therefore salt is good." Where was Jesus going now? In the Lord's mind, what is good is living life in fellowship with him where we offer everything to him. As you follow this Jesus you become very salty! You add pungency to this planet. People who aren't afraid to follow Jesus as he works in their families, in their workplaces, in their social circles, in their church fellowships and in the planet at large add true flavor to this world. God doesn't make cookie cutter Christians. That is something religious legalism does to us.

The point is if salt loses its unique flavor it's useless for its intended purpose. It's not good for seasoning, it's not good for the soil, it's not even good for manure. Jesus called us the salt of the world. We keep that saltiness by following him. He is free from the bonds of this world. He broke through death at the cross and freed us from its grip. Jesus calls to us and encourages us not to be afraid. Let him have what you've got. He'll take care of it. He may add to it. He may enrich it. He may have a bigger idea for your life than you could have thought possible. The opposite of saltiness is blandness. The Lord has better things in mind for us than that.

To become the salt that God intends us to be, we need the work of the cross in our lives. Our natural inclination is toward security and safety. We don't want to face the possibility of rejection. We don't want to risk looking stupid. On top of that, the enemy seeks to lull us into complacency with earthly distractions. Many opt for a Jesus who saves them from their sins but isn't allowed to be too active in their lives. From Jesus' point of view, that kind of Christian living doesn't add much flavor to the earth. The more we live in fellowship with him, the more flavorful our lives become. How do we get there from here? We follow Jesus. We surrender our lives to the Jesus who went to the cross and yet lives again. Following the crucified Christ has a cost. But you will get more in return than you could ever imagine.

The Cross Unleashes Jesus

Believers know that Jesus died on the cross for their sins, but many aren't sure how the work of the cross practically impacts their lives. Paul explained this in several New Testament passages. In I Corinthians 1:17-19 Paul writes, "Christ did not send me to baptize, but to preach the gospel, not in cleverness of speech, that the cross of Christ should not be made void. For the word of the cross is to those who are perishing foolishness, but to us who are being saved it is the power of God."

The Corinthians were dividing themselves according to various workers who had come to Corinth. To counter that, Paul said his primary mission was preaching the gospel in such a way that the message of the cross wouldn't lose its teeth. He reminded them that it appeared stupid to talk to people about the cross. The Lord Jesus encountered that with Peter when Peter pulled him aside and told him not to go to the cross. But Paul had come to understand that all are perishing due to sin, and that outside of the cross there is no way to deal with that sin. He admitted this sounded foolish to those who would rather play lofty mind games about the goodness of man, or the origin of the universe. But they were perishing! So Paul thundered out that the message of the cross was the power of God for those who were being saved.

The cross turns loose the power of God because the cross unleashed Jesus Christ to become the life-giving Spirit. Paul put it this way: "The first Adam became a living soul, the last Adam a life-giving spirit." Jesus Christ died on the cross as the Son of Man. He was resurrected by the eternal Spirit and, as Paul put it in Romans 1:4, "he was declared the Son of God with power by the resurrection from the dead, according to the Spirit of holiness, Jesus Christ our Lord." After his resurrection Jesus ascended into the heavens and was glorified. Then he re-entered the physical world with the ability to breathe his Spirit into those who would receive him. The cross unleashes the power of God into your life when you receive Jesus. When we preach Christ crucified, we also preach Christ resurrected, the power of God and the wisdom of God. As the life-giving Spirit, he wants to set us free from death; free from pride; free from sin; free from loneliness and fear; free to live a fruitful life.

No More Body Casts

When my wife was a teen-ager, she had a curved spine, known as scoliosis. To solve that problem, doctors put her in a body cast. The cast extended from her neck to her waist and she wore it for a year. Somehow the mere presence of that cast was supposed to change the direction of her spine. Sadly, it did not. It was not very comfortable or attractive, but she wore it, having been promised that it might do some good.

This may be the way many view the work of the cross. When it comes to applying the cross to their lives, many think God wants to put them in a body cast. They fear he is going to saddle them with one list of things they have to do and another list of things they can't do. Or he is going to find ways to make them suffer so that they can be better people in the end. Because they think it's for their own good, the really devout say, "Okay God, bring on the cross, bring on the body cast." The rest run for cover.

If you can relate to that mindset, take heart. That is not how God works the benefits of the cross into your life. The fact is that without Jesus, people are already in a body cast and don't know what to do about it. They want to soar, but they can't. They have the sense that they were made for something eternal, but they don't know how to fulfill that longing. They are bound up with sin, with guilt, with a fear of rejection, with shame, and with an impending fear that inevitably death waits out there for them. Though they may find ways to live with and cover over their inadequacies, a yearning to be free remains in their hearts. The fact is that they are in body casts. They were created for higher things, but they have been bound by an enemy who managed to alienate them from the God who made them.

If you've had such a mindset, Jesus Christ wants to cut you out of your body cast and set you free through his death on the cross. The cross released Jesus Christ to enter the lives of his followers and set them free from all that binds them. As Paul wrote to the Romans, "Therefore there is now no condemnation for those who are in Christ Jesus. For the law of the Spirit of life in Christ Jesus has set you free from the law of sin and of death" (Romans 8:1-2). Through his death on the cross, the Lord Jesus freed us from sin and death; now the work of the cross in our lives is to come in and to cut away what remains of the body cast. "It was for freedom that Christ set us free" (Galatians 5:1).

Does That Hurt?

Yes. It can. Oftentimes the process of setting us free is painful. But much of life contains pain. So why not opt for the pain that leads to healing. The Lord faces obstacles in transforming us into his image. Our pride stands in the way. Our flesh stands in the way. Our selfishness stands in the way. Our old habits stand in the way.

On my first visit to India I was driving in a rented vehicle with two other believers to visit an interior village where a church had been planted. I was to speak that night to the believers there, many of whom had traveled a fair distance to attend the meeting. It was a very rainy night as the monsoon season had begun. As the driver went through one of the towns on the way to the village, he had to go around a large bus standing on the road side.

As we reached the front of the bus an elderly man stepped out in front of our car. There was no way our driver could miss him. When the car hit him he was launched over the hood directly into the windshield. The large wooden staff that he carried smashed into the glass, shattering it. The man flipped over the car and landed in the ditch behind us. The driver immediately pulled over. As I was sitting on that side of the car I opened my door and looked back at the man. He lay there in the ditch with his face covered in blood. His beseeching eyes looked into mine as if to say, "Why are you here? Why did you do this to me?"

Immediately the driver pulled away from the curb and sped away from the scene. I was shocked. I was sure we would stay and help the man. But the driver was not going to put his life in jeopardy at the hands of what could become an angry mob. We drove on out of the town and into the surrounding forested countryside. The pouring rain flooded in through the broken front windshield. The men around me clamored at one another in a language I could not understand. All I could think about was that this old man had likely been killed and that was on my shoulders. If I had not been there, that car would never have been traveling through that town at that moment.

We continued to the village. When we arrived the driver dropped us off and sped away. Our meeting with the villagers went on as if nothing had happened. Still, I was in shock trying to absorb what had transpired.

We ended up catching a local bus after the meeting ended and making our way back to the hotel where I was staying. I really couldn't process well what had happened so I stuffed my emotions down deep inside and went on with the rest of the trip.

My first night back at home I lay in bed thinking about that event. My emotions finally came to the surface. Though I still do not fully understand why such things happen, I began to sob. "Why Lord? Why did that happen? How could I have caused the death of that man?" I remember the Lord's response, "I'm going to use this to break your heart for India." I really didn't even know what that meant. But as I lay there in my distress, I surrendered. "OK, Lord, if that is what you want." I accepted what happened as from the Lord. At that point in time I had no idea that I would return many times to India and form lifelong friendships there. For me, trusting Jesus with that pain was an experience of taking up the cross. Why did the Lord allow that into my life? For one thing, that experience caused a deeper compassion to grow in my heart for the people and culture of India than was there before. That helped me as I strove to build loving friendships with many Indian believers. To bring things full circle, for three years I carried guilt over that man's death. Then one day in speaking with one of the Indian men who had been in the car that night, I found out that the man had survived. He had been taken to a hospital and had recovered. What a relief! Thank you Lord.

Is Life Always Fair?

That is a rather dramatic example of the Lord using suffering to change a life. Many, many of us have stories about how such unbidden pain has helped shape our lives. But there are many ways both large and small that the Lord has to shape us through the cross. Some of them are hidden. Suppose we are wronged by someone or are unfairly maligned. We want to get even; we want to strike back. But we have an inner checking. We feel the Lord is asking us to let it go. But our insides cry out, "But it's not fair. No one will know I've been wronged. No one will know I laid down my life." To that the Lord replies, "I will know." And so we say,

OK, Lord and lay it down. In that moment we suffer a small death to our soul. On the other side of that death, however, we find new liberty and increased peace as we become less self-conscious and more conscious of the goodness and wisdom of God. That's why Paul said to the Romans, "The mind set on the flesh is death, but the mind set on the Spirit is life and peace" (Romans 8:6).

The cross turned Jesus Christ loose so that you could receive him. He, in turn, imparts his life to you. Our part in that includes saying, "Yes, Lord, go ahead. Turn loose the power of the cross in me." At times it will hurt. Death is operating in you. But the operation ends in life. Paul made this clear to the Corinthians when he wrote, "For we who live are constantly being delivered over to death for Jesus' sake, so that the life of Jesus also may be manifested in our mortal flesh. So death works in us, but life in you" (II Corinthians 4: 11-12). The phrase "for Jesus' sake" actually refers to the deadening power of Jesus that he exerts in us in order to produce new life. We are delivered over to death by Jesus just as a patient is turned over to a skilled surgeon to cut away cancerous growths that were keeping life from flourishing. Though painful, those who have tasted his life know that this is a result worth the surgery.

The message of the cross is ultimately one of simplicity. It's not complicated. Receive by faith the reality that Jesus' death was sufficient to cover your sins. Turn over to him the authority to set you free. The realization will follow that his love for you is great and that he does that which is in your eternal best interests. As you submit to his loving work of molding you into his image, he begins the process of setting you free.

Freed from Outward Performance

So what does true freedom look like? And how should we behave while God is working on us? Many believe that certain behaviors automatically go along with being "Christian." There are things we have to do. You can make your own list here of what those behaviors are. We feel compelled to do them, even though internally our lives are in disarray. Paul addressed this problem when he wrote to the Galatians when circumcision was being forced on them as one of those necessary behaviors, "Those who desire to make a good showing in the flesh try to compel you to be circumcised, simply so that they will not be persecuted for the cross of Christ…but may it never be that I would boast, except in the cross of our Lord Jesus Christ, through which the world has been crucified to me, and I to the world" (Galatians 6:12-14). The believers in Galatia were being told that while Christ was good, there were certain outward rites that they also needed to observe (i.e., circumcision, observation of certain special days, etc.) if they wanted to please God.

Paul fought against this false teaching by explaining to them that at the cross of Christ they were set free from being on a performance basis with God and others. The cross proclaims that none will ever be good enough to satisfy God with outward performance. It took the death of Christ and his resurrection presence in us to make us acceptable to God. Paul knew only too well that he had been released from all the expectations that the Law, his religion and his culture had laid on him regarding what it meant to be acceptable before God. He was a free man, and he wasn't going back to old ways of living. He was determined to lead as many others into freedom as possible. That world of blindness and captivity had been separated from him by the death and resurrection of his Lord. Its power to keep him in darkness was broken.

As he wrote to the Colossians, "See to it that no one takes you captive through philosophy and empty deception, according to the tradition of men, according to the elementary principles of the world, rather than according to Christ" (Colossians 2:8). Paul had had enough of the hollow pride that comes from looking good on the outside. He would only boast in the wonderful work of Christ at the cross that had freed him from having to make an outward show and whose effective work in him actually did produce the fruit of peaceful living. The day of Christ's death on the cross marked our true independence day. We should view it as such.

How to View the Cross

Let's take a look at two amazing perspectives on the cross. We'll start with Paul. Here is what he wrote to the Philippians: "I count all things to be loss in view of the surpassing value of knowing Christ Jesus my

Lord, for whom I have suffered the loss of all things, and count them but refuse so that I may gain Christ...that I may know him and the power of his resurrection and the fellowship of his sufferings, being conformed to his death; in order that I may attain to the resurrection from the dead" (Philippians 3:8, 10-11).

These are stirring and challenging words. In this section of Philippians, Paul listed all the things that he could have boasted in. While there were many, he counted them all worthless in comparison to what he found in his pursuit of the Lord Jesus. He suffered much but counted that suffering as light when compared to the glory that waited ahead. He wrote to the Corinthians, "For momentary, light affliction is producing for us an eternal weight of glory far beyond all comparison" (II Corinthians 4:17). Without hesitation he invited all who would read his words to follow him in surrendering his life to Christ.

He did that because he was in love. Consider his words, "For the love of Christ controls us, having concluded this, that one died for all, therefore all died; and he died for all, so that they who live might no longer live for themselves, but for him who died and rose again on their behalf" (II Corinthians 5:14-15). Paul was in love with the Lord Jesus. He had come to understand how much the Lord loved him, even to the point of surrendering his life for Paul. That love had been poured into Paul's heart through the Spirit. Now that same love that motivated God the Father to send his Son Jesus to the cross was working in Paul. Paul wanted all those with whom he came in contact to be freed by the Lord Jesus as he had been. He knew the road to freedom ran through the cross. But we don't start with embracing the cross. We start by experiencing the love that Jesus has for us and feeling love for him grow in our own hearts. That's what makes us willing to be worked on by him.

But many in Paul's world were opposed to God's people being set free. They derided the message of the cross and the promise of life that lay beyond it. They were effectively closing the door to the riches that Jesus Christ died to make available to those who would receive him. Their impact so distressed Paul that it moved him to tears. He went on to write, "For many walk, of whom I often told you and now tell you even weeping, that they are enemies of the cross of Christ whose end is destruction...who set their minds on earthly things. For our citizenship is in the heavens, from which also we eagerly wait for a Savior, the Lord Jesus Christ" (Philippians 3:18-20).

The enemies of the cross would rather people be destroyed than experience the gift of life made available in Jesus. At one time Paul was among them. But he had tasted the air of the heavens, and a whole new world had opened up to him. Now his heart of love for the Lord and his people motivated Paul to declare the wonders of his crucified Jesus and the freedom found at the cross. He wept that so many would want to close the way to the path of life, and he encouraged those who loved the Lord to hold fast to him. May the Lord fill our understanding with such a perspective and our hearts with such a love.

Who for the Joy...

Our final look at the cross centers on the one who bore its terrible pain for us, the Lord Jesus. Most believers are familiar with the Lord's actions on the night he was crucified. He arranged for one final meal with his closest friends before he headed for Gethsemane where he was betrayed. At that meal the Lord took bread, broke it into pieces and offered it to his followers. He then took a cup of wine and offered that to them as well. Here's how Matthew described the scene: "Now as they were eating, Jesus took bread and praising God, gave thanks ... and when he had broken it, he gave it to the disciples and said, Take, eat; this is my body. And he took a cup, and when he had given thanks, he gave it to them, saying, Drink of it, all of you; For this is My blood of the new covenant, which is being poured out for many for the forgiveness of sins" (Matthew 26: 26-28 Amplified Bible).

Jesus knew that the purpose for which he came to this planet was at hand. He knew that an excruciating and humiliating death was only hours away. He knew that the sin and shame of humanity was about to be laid on his shoulders. Still, as he picked up the bread that represented his own body, he did something truly amazing. He praised and thanked his Father. How could he do that, knowing what lay ahead?

He could be thankful that his own body would be broken for only one reason: He knew it would free him up to be received by you! "This is my body, it's for you," is how the Lord explained those events to Paul in I Corinthians 11: 24. Jesus did the same thing with the cup that represented his blood. In that blood a new covenant would be born, one that is based on his righteousness made available to us. If you have received him, you have experienced the freedom found in having your slate with God wiped clean.

But Jesus wasn't done showing us how to approach the cross. "And singing a hymn, they went out to the Mount of Olives" (Matthew 26:30, Concordant Literal New Testament). Where did Christians learn to sing in the face of adversity? Such activity was born in that circle of friends by Jesus himself as he faced the greatest challenge in all of time and eternity. Heading towards the most excruciating death known to man, the sinless Lord gathered his band of soon-to-be brothers around him and showed them how to face trials.

He began to sing.

The Lord, who had already praised and thanked his Father for what was about to be unleashed through his death and resurrection, knew what they did not: that his God was about to unloose the cords of death that had bound mankind almost since the day of creation. He knew that because of what he was about to endure the whole family of God would come to experience the love, oneness and fellowship with his Father that he experienced. He knew that, energized by his Spirit, they would go out in his Name and offer that love to those who don't know it.

As he considered the freedom and life that was soon to be made available to those with him in that room—and one day to you and me—that brought him joy. He must have dreaded what lay immediately before him. His soul screamed within him to try and escape the coming wrath. We know that from his words in the garden of Gethsemane, "Father, if it be possible, let this cup pass from me," and from the blood that he sweated as he prayed there. Nonetheless, as he considered it all, the joy of what was set before him rose to the surface, and Jesus began to sing.

What song could have been on his lips? Maybe it was a declaration of God's closeness, as a song taken from Psalm 32 describes: "You are my hiding place, you always fill my heart with songs of deliverance, whenever I am afraid, I will trust in you." Perhaps it was a prayer of dependence, as in Psalm 25: "Unto you, O Lord, do I lift up my soul; oh my God, I trust in you, let me not be ashamed, let not my enemies triumph over me." It could have been a song declaring the reality of what was about to take place based on Psalm 125: "When the LORD brought back the captive ones of Zion, we were like those who dream. Then our mouth was filled with laughter and our tongue with joyful shouting; then they said among the nations, The LORD has done great things for them. The LORD has done great things for us; we are glad. Restore our captivity, O LORD, as the streams in the South. Those who sow in tears shall reap with joyful shouting. He, who goes to and fro weeping, carrying his bag of seed, shall indeed come again with a shout of joy, bringing his sheaves with him."

The Lord led his disciples to the place of his betrayal singing. What a Savior! He could go to the cross in this way because he knew a loving Father was waiting for him with open arms on the other side In God's wondrous plan, we were included in that death. As Paul put it so beautifully, "Do you not know that all of us who have been baptized into Christ Jesus have been baptized into his death? Therefore, we have been buried with him through baptism into death, in order that as Christ was raised from the dead through the glory of the Father, so we too might walk in newness of life" (Romans 6:3-4). Now that loving Father waits for us, as well. Newness of life in his presence awaits all who are willing to pick up their cross and follow the Lord Jesus.

If God has touched your heart by the powerful work of the cross, this is a good time to stop and thank him for the work done there. His intention is to set you free through his power unleashed at the cross. The work of the cross unleashes the divine power of God for salvation and brings defeat to God's enemy. May it be so in our experience.